The LBC Cookbook

Michelle Berriedale-Johnson

A Martin Book

Published by Martin Books
an imprint of Woodhead-Faulkner Limited
Fitzwilliam House, 32 Trumpington Street, Cambridge CB2 1QY

First published 1985
Text © Michelle Berriedale-Johnson 1985
Illustrations © Woodhead-Faulkner (Publishers) Ltd 1985

British Library Cataloguing in Publication Data
Berriedale-Johnson, Michelle
   The LBC cookbook.
   1. Cookery
   I. Title
   641.5   TX717

   ISBN 0-85941-338-1

Design and layout: Geoff Green
Cover design: Peter Walker
Cover photograph: Julie Fisher
Illustrations: Philippa Shanks
Typesetting: Hands Fotoset, Leicester
Printed by St Edmundsbury Press, Bury St Edmunds, Suffolk

Contents

The Author

Michelle Berriedale-Johnson has written cookery books on subjects as diverse as seventeenth century Pepysian cooking and how to rescue culinary disasters! When not writing or broadcasting, she runs a successful catering business, Catercall Ltd, in central London; demonstrates and teaches historical and contemporary English cooking in the United Kingdom and America; and acts as historical food consultant to the English Tourist Board, the BBC and many film and television companies. She is frequently on television and radio. Michelle is a history graduate from Trinity College, Dublin.

Note

Ingredients are given in both metric and imperial quantities, and you should use either set, but not a mixture of both, in any one recipe. Egg size is size 3 (medium) unless otherwise stated.

Introduction

The recipes in this book have been chosen from those broadcast on LBC's AM programme since I joined it in 1983. Since AM is above all a topical programme, my recipes too aim for topicality rather than pursuing any particular theme. Thus you should expect to get Irish stew on St Patrick's day, strawberry recipes in June, turkey around Christmas time and a hangover cure on New Year's Day! You may also find yourself with the occasional oddity such as a 'dishwashered salmon', 'flea fudge' or a recipe inspired by a guest, a joke or any of our travels.

But although there is no obvious link between the recipes I devise for LBC, all my cooking is based on a 'healthy' approach to food and eating. I am not a vegetarian, nor am I in any way doctrinaire about what I eat and cook. I do believe, however, that fresh vegetables, wholemeal flour and a restricted intake of sugar, junk food and additives are better for you – and make you feel better – than a diet of white bread, burgers, chips and ice cream.

Nonetheless, I accept that even the healthiest of eaters has a gastronomic Achilles heel, and although I am blissfully happy for weeks on end with salads and brown bread, yogurt and fresh fruit, bean pots and fish, I do have the occasional desperate craving for a hunk of gooey, calorific and thoroughly unhealthy chocolate gâteau! So for those of us who feel that the occasional sin only makes our virtues shine more brightly I have included a few luscious but definitely not healthfood recipes.

Because it proved so popular with listeners, I have also included the contents of the Simply Simple booklet which we distributed in the winters of 1983/4 and 84/5. These were easy and cheap but nutritious and tasty recipes designed primarily for old age pensioners and people with physical problems such as lack of mobility or arthritic hands. They also worked well, however, for those who disliked cooking or found themselves with restricted cooking facilities, such as a hot ring in a cupboard.

I hope you enjoy the recipes in the book. I have certainly had enormous fun compiling and – thanks to the AM team both front and backstage – broadcasting them.

Soups

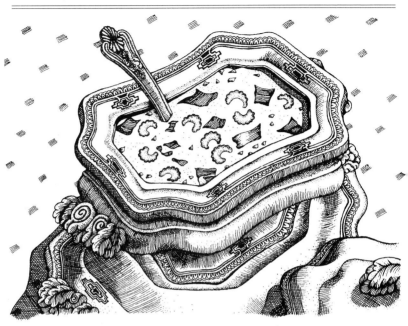

Chilled cucumber and radish soup

Serves 6
Broadcast 7 July 1984

The pink and white of grated radish is remarkably pretty either in a salad, or, as I have used it here, as part of a soup.

1 medium-size cucumber

12 large spring onions

juice of 2 lemons

300 ml/½ pint natural low-fat yogurt

300 ml/½ pint milk

10 large radishes, grated finely

a few drops of Tabasco sauce

sea salt

Purée the unpeeled cucumbers with the spring onions in a food processor or liquidiser. Turn the mixture into a bowl and stir in the lemon juice, milk and yogurt. Season to taste with sea salt and a little Tabasco sauce. Add the grated radish and chill thoroughly before serving.

Eliza Smith's fasting day soup

Serves 6
Broadcast
21 April 1983

In 1983, Arlon House Publishing brought out a facsimile of the 1758 edition of Eliza Smith's Compleat Housewife or Gentlewoman's Companion. Naturally, I had to get a copy and then had a hard job choosing this recipe from the many hundreds that Eliza had on offer. It is called a 'fasting day soup' as it contains neither meat nor meat stock and so could be eaten on 'fast days'. If sorrel is not available, just increase the quantity of spinach to 100 g/4 oz.

25 g/1 oz butter or low-fat margarine

50 g/2 oz fresh spinach, washed and chopped roughly

50 g/2 oz fresh sorrel, washed and chopped roughly

a small handful of roughly chopped parsley

¼ small lettuce, chopped

1 small onion stuck with 12 cloves

25 g/1 oz fresh whole-meal breadcrumbs

25 g/1 oz pistachio nuts, shelled

1200 ml/2 pints water

2 egg yolks

4 tablespoons dry white wine

juice of 1 lemon

salt and black pepper

In a pan, melt the butter and lightly cook the spinach, sorrel, parsley and lettuce for 5 minutes or until they are well wilted. Add the onion stuck with the cloves, the breadcrumbs, pistachio nuts, water and a little salt and pepper. Bring to the boil and simmer for 20 minutes. Remove the onion and purée the soup in a liquidiser or food processor, then strain it through a coarse sieve and return it to the pan. Whisk the egg yolks with the wine and lemon juice, then whisk the mixture into the soup. Cook gently for a couple of minutes (but do not boil) and serve immediately.

Mulligatawny soup

Serves 6
Broadcast
5 January 1984

1 small onion

1 small carrot

half a small turnip

1 stick of celery

1 small apple

25 g/1 oz butter

50 g/2 oz ham, diced

2 cloves

a sprig of parsley

1 bayleaf

1/2 teaspoon dried thyme

1/2 tablespoon curry powder

25 g/1 oz flour

1/2 tablespoon curry paste

1.2 litres/2 pints chicken stock

900 ml/6 fl oz medium-dry sherry

salt and pepper

Prepare and finely chop the vegetables and apple. Melt the butter in a large pan and gently fry the vegetables, apple, ham, cloves, and herbs for 5 minutes without burning. Mix the curry powder with the flour and mix both into the curry paste. Add this to the vegetables and cook for a couple of minutes before adding the stock. Bring to the boil and simmer for 30 minutes. Remove the soup from the heat and purée it; return it to the pan, add the sherry and season to taste with salt and pepper. Reheat to serve.

Traditionally, the soup is served with small pieces of cooked chicken floating in it, and a bowl of plain boiled rice.

Nettle soup

Serves 4
Broadcast
21 August 1983

If you happen to be in the country in spring when young nettles are sprouting, take some rubber gloves and pick a bagful; they make a delicious and very nutritious soup, being high in minerals like all green leaf vegetables. Discard the stalks before using.

25 g/1 oz butter or low-fat margarine

75 g/3 oz onions, peeled and sliced roughly

Melt the butter or margarine in a pan and lightly fry the onions until they begin to soften. Add the nettles and lettuce and stir around for a couple of minutes. Then add

8

75 g/3 oz young nettle tops and leaves, washed

half a cabbage lettuce, chopped

600 ml/1 pint good chicken stock

50 g/2 oz fresh whole-meal breadcrumbs

juice of 1 orange

juice of ½ lemon

salt and freshly ground black pepper

the stock and the breadcrumbs, bring to the boil and allow to simmer for 30 minutes. Purée the soup in a liquidiser, food processor or blender and then return it to the pan. Add the orange and lemon juice and season to taste with salt and freshly ground black pepper. You can serve this either hot or cold.

Bermuda onion soup

Serves 6
Broadcast
21 March 1985

This was the result of a brief week in Bermuda advising on a new English restaurant there. Bermudan fish was wonderful but astronomically expensive and almost unobtainable – so I settled for the onion soup! Bermudan onions are large and very sweet; the nearest we can get here are the big spanish ones.

40 g/1½ oz butter

1 tablespoon olive oil

450 g/1 lb sweet spanish onions, peeled and sliced thinly

1 tablespoon chopped fresh thyme or ½ tablespoon dried thyme

900 ml/1½ pints chicken stock

4–6 half-slices of close-grained wholemeal bread

100–175 g/4–6 oz well-flavoured Cheddar cheese, grated

salt and freshly ground black pepper

Melt the butter and oil in a heavy-based saucepan, add the onions and thyme and sweat them gently, without burning, for 30 minutes. Add the chicken stock and a little salt and pepper and simmer for a further 30–40 minutes. Adjust the seasoning to taste. Spoon the soup into bowls and put a slice of bread on the top of each. Sprinkle the cheese generously over the top of the bread and brown it under a hot grill for 4–5 minutes. Eat at once with a little extra freshly ground black pepper if you like.

Pink rhubarb soup for spring

Serves 6
Broadcast
10 February 1983

50 g/2 oz butter or low-fat margarine

450 g/1 lb young rhubarb, trimmed and chopped roughly

50 g/2 oz young leek, cleaned and sliced finely

25 g/1 oz cooked lean ham, chopped small

50 g/2 oz fresh whole-meal breadcrumbs

1.2 litres/2 pints chicken or light veal stock

150 ml/¼ pint dry white wine

a couple of drops of Tabasco sauce

juice of a small lemon

3–4 teaspoons brown or granulated sugar

150 ml/¼ pint double cream, whipped lightly, or 150 ml/¼ pint set natural yogurt

salt

Melt the butter in a saucepan, then add the rhubarb, leek and ham and stew them gently for 10 minutes or until the rhubarb is soft. Add the breadcrumbs, stock and wine, bring them to the boil and simmer for 15 minutes. Liquidise or purée the soup and return it to the pan. Add the salt, Tabasco, lemon juice and sugar to taste; how much of the last two you add will depend on how sweet the rhubarb and your own tooth is! You can use brown or white sugar, but remember that brown will add some colour to the soup. Reheat gently and serve with a blob of whipped cream or yogurt in the middle of each bowl.

Chilled green pepper and prawn soup

Serves 4
Broadcast 23 June 1983

This soup is something of a luxury as, sadly, whole prawns are not cheap. But it is delicious and worth splashing out on for a summer dinner party.

6 spring onions

100 g/4 oz cooked prawns in their shells

150 ml/5 fl oz natural low-fat yogurt

300 ml/10 fl oz milk

juice of 1 lemon

1 stick of celery, chopped *very* finely

1 medium-size green pepper, cored, de-seeded and chopped finely

6 drops of Tabasco sauce

salt and white pepper

Clean and roughly chop 2 spring onions and put them in a pan with 300 ml/10 fl oz water. Shell the prawns and add the shells to the onions and water. Bring them to the boil and simmer for 25 minutes, then cool and strain the liquid.

Mix the yogurt and milk in a bowl and slowly add the lemon juice. Add the celery, green pepper and remaining spring onions, cleaned and chopped finely. Then add the prawns and Tabasco sauce. Pour in the cooled fish stock, stir well together and put in the fridge to chill for a couple of hours. Take out of the fridge, stir again, season to taste with salt and white pepper and return to the fridge for another couple of hours before serving, for the flavours to combine really thoroughly.

Starters, light lunches and supper dishes

Spinach and mushroom pâté

Serves 8
Broadcast
7 February 1985

Although this is a vegetarian recipe, it should also appeal to non-vegetarians who find the traditional fish and meat-based pâtés unmanageably rich. It freezes very well.

450 g/1 lb fresh spinach

225 g/8 oz leeks, trimmed and sliced finely

40 g/1½ oz butter or low-fat margarine

225 g/8 oz open mushrooms with their stems, cleaned and chopped roughly

40 g/1½ oz pumpkin or sunflower seeds

Wash the spinach, remove the coarsest stems and cook it in just the water which clings to its leaves for 8–10 minutes on a hob or 3–4 minutes in a microwave. Drain the spinach thoroughly, squashing out any excess liquid with a spoon, and chop it roughly.

Meanwhile, soften the leeks in the butter or margarine, then add the mushrooms and cook both together for 3–4 minutes. Add the chopped spinach, the pumpkin or sunflower seeds, breadcrumbs and the

12

75 g/3 oz fresh wholemeal breadcrumbs

1 egg

salt and pepper

egg. Mix the whole lot thoroughly together and season to taste with salt and black pepper.

Pack the mixture into a loaf tin, a loose-bottomed cake tin, or a soufflé dish; if you want to be sure of getting it out easily it would be wise to line the dish with foil or greaseproof paper. Cover it and bake it in a moderate oven (180°C/350°F/Gas Mark 4) for 30 minutes. Take it out of the oven, let it cool slightly, then weight it and allow it to cool completely. Turn it out and serve it with wholemeal toast or crackers.

Tomato fondue

Serves 4
Broadcast
23 April 1983

For those who find a real cheese fondue rather rich, this makes an excellent substitute. You can make it with fresh tomatoes but the flavour is slightly less definite and you have to skin them.

25 g/1 oz butter or low-fat margarine

1 small onion, chopped finely

2 cloves of garlic, crushed

800 g/28 oz can of tomatoes, drained

1 teaspoon dried oregano

2 teaspoons dried basil

300 ml/½ pint dry white wine or lager

450 g/1 lb well-flavoured Cheddar cheese, grated

1 teaspoon french mustard

salt and pepper

Melt the butter or margarine in a fondue dish or flameproof casserole and gently cook the onion and garlic until they are soft but not coloured. Mash the tomatoes to a pulp and add them to the onion and garlic. Add the herbs and the wine or lager. Bring the mixture to the boil and simmer for 10 minutes. If you like a very smooth fondue, put the mixture through a food processor or liquidiser at this point, then add the remaining ingredients. If you prefer a rougher texture, just add the cheese and mustard and continue to cook until the cheese is melted. Check the seasoning and serve at once, dipping wholemeal bread cubes into the fondue on the end of a fork.

Guacamole

If, rather than rock-hard avocados, you find yourself with very squashy and discoloured ones, turn them into a guacamole – a classic Mexican dish, which is very easy to make.

4 very ripe avocados, peeled, stoned and puréed

1 small onion, peeled and chopped *very* finely

1–2 cloves of garlic to taste, peeled and crushed

2 firm tomatoes, skinned, de-seeded and chopped finely

4–6 black olives, stoned and chopped finely

about 2 tablespoons lemon juice

several drops of Tabasco sauce

If the avocados are really ripe you should be able to purée them with a wooden spoon in a bowl. Add the onion and garlic and mix well, then fold in the tomatoes and as many olives as you like. Season to taste with the lemon juice and Tabasco sauce; you probably will not need any further seasoning as the olives are sufficiently salty and the Tabasco sufficiently fiery to make anything more 'de trop'! Serve the guacamole as a dip with crudités or Mexican corn tortilla chips (if you can find them), or as a pâté with hot, wholemeal toast.

Take care to cover the guacamole tightly if it is not to be used immediately as, like all avocado dishes, it will lose its colour if exposed to the air.

Cheese and mustard 'pudding'

A real warming winter dish, perfect for eating on your knees in front of the TV. Also a good way of using up stale bread and old cheese!

50 g/2 oz butter or low-fat margarine

4 thick slices of wholemeal bread

2 tablespoons made mustard

Grease a 20 cm/8-inch pie dish well with the butter or margarine. Spread both sides of the bread with the remains of the butter and the mustard which can be English, French, or a wholegrain or herbed one. Put two slices in the bottom of the pie dish and

175 g/6 oz well-flavoured Cheddar cheese, grated

4 eggs

175 ml/6 fl oz real ale, white wine, chicken or vegetable stock or milk

salt and freshly ground black pepper

cover these with half the cheese, then the other two slices of bread. Whisk the eggs with the ale (with English mustard), white wine (with the others), stock or milk and season them *lightly* with salt and pepper. Pour this liquid over the bread (as though you were making bread and butter pudding) and sprinkle over the remains of the cheese. Bake in a moderate oven (180°C/ 350°F/Gas Mark 4) for 25–30 minutes or until the pudding is puffed, set and golden on top.

Serve it at once with a little extra freshly ground black pepper.

Mushrooms stuffed with Gorgonzola and spinach

Serves 6
Broadcast 30 June 1984

You can make this with button mushrooms, but the flavour of the flat field ones is so much better that it is worth a bit of an effort to find them. You can also cook the dish in a microwave, but you will not then get the cheese to brown.

450 g/1 lb large flat mushrooms

about 25 g/1 oz butter or low-fat margarine

225 g/8 oz fresh spinach

340 g/12 oz ripe Gorgonzola or dolcelatte cheese, grated

6 slices wholewheat toast

freshly ground black pepper

Take the stalks out of the mushrooms and dot the shells with a little melted butter or low-fat margarine. Put them under a grill until the butter is melted and the mushrooms slightly cooked. Meanwhile, chop the spinach fairly small and mix it thoroughly with the cheese. Fill the mushrooms with the mixture and put them back under the grill for 2–3 minutes or until the cheese is melted and lightly browned.

Eat them at once either with or on the wholewheat toast, with some freshly ground black pepper.

Broad bean tart

Serves 8
Broadcast
4 August 1983

This recipe comes from my Olde Englishe Recipe Book and it is perfect for the young broad beans which should be available in early summer. The original recipe of 1695 tells you to layer the beans 'with wet sweetmeats as of Apples, Abricocks, Peaches, Plums, Pears and etc. and between each layer to strew a little sugar . . . ' I have amended it slightly!

150 g/5 oz wholemeal flour

40 g/1½ oz butter or low-fat margarine

40 g/1½ oz lard

225 g/8 oz fresh, young broad beans, shelled

3 eggs

1 teaspoon wholegrain mustard

½ teaspoon dark brown sugar

100 g/4 oz tart eating apples, peeled and diced

100 g/4 oz lean ham, diced

300 ml/½ pint cider

salt and pepper

Rub the fats into the pastry and add cold water to make a firm dough. Roll out the pastry and line a 20 cm/8-inch flan dish. Line the dish with foil, weight it with beans or rice and bake it blind; it should take about 30 minutes in a moderate oven (190°C/375°F/Gas Mark 5). Remove the foil and beans 5–10 minutes before it is cooked, to crisp up the base. Turn the oven down to 150°C/300°F/Gas Mark 2.

Meanwhile, cook the beans in some lightly salted water until they are just tender, but take care not to overcook them. In a bowl, beat the eggs with the mustard, sugar and seasoning. Add the beans, diced apple and ham, then the cider and mix all thoroughly together. Pour the mixture into the flan case and bake in a slow oven for about 50 minutes or until the custard is set. Serve warm, but not hot.

Rempah-rempah udang (beansprout and prawn fritters)

Serves 4–6
Broadcast
17 November 1983

Sri Owen, the well-known Indonesian cook, came into the studios one morning to give us a touch of the exotic east. Her prawn fritters can be served as a snack with a drink or as a side dish with a rice meal, and are not even difficult to make!

100 g/4 oz shelled or frozen prawns, chopped or minced

4 spring onions, chopped finely

100 g/4 oz beansprouts, cleaned

50 g/2 oz rice flour or self-raising white flour

1 teaspoon baking powder

2 tablespoons each chopped chives and parsley

3 tablespoons coarsely ground fresh or dessicated coconut

2 cloves of garlic, crushed

1 teaspoon ground ginger

1/2 teaspoon chilli powder

2 large eggs (size 1–2), beaten

vegetable or groundnut oil for frying

salt and pepper

Put the prawns, spring onions and beansprouts into a bowl. Sift the flour and baking powder into them, then add the herbs, coconut, garlic and spices and mix them all together well. Beat the eggs, season them with salt and pepper and fold them into the mixture; if it is a little dry add a tablespoon of cold water. Form it lightly into walnut-size balls and then flatten these into burger shapes. Deep-fry in hot oil for 1½–2 minutes or until they are golden brown all over. The rempah-rempah udang can be served hot or cold or reheated in a moderate oven, (180°C/350°F/Gas Mark 4) before serving. This dish is not, however, suitable for reheating in a microwave.

A herb and bacon pie

Serves 8
Broadcast
17 November 1984

This is another of my old English dishes and is particularly tasty if you can get fresh herbs. You alter the quantities and kinds of the vegetables or herbs according to your own taste or what is available.

150 g/5 oz wholewheat flour or wholewheat and plain white flour mixed

40 g/1½ oz butter

40 g/1½ oz lard or vegetable shortening

450 g/1 lb lean bacon rashers, sliced thinly

225 g/8 oz leeks, chopped finely

225 g/8 oz fresh spinach, chopped finely

1 carton of mustard and cress

a bunch of fresh watercress

a large handful of roughly chopped parsley

the leaves from 2 sprigs each of fresh thyme and savory, chopped

2 sage leaves, chopped

3 eggs

150 ml/¼ pint chicken stock

salt and pepper

Cut the fats into the flour, then rub them in until the mixture is really crumbly. Add enough cold water to make a firm dough and set aside.

Remove the rind from the bacon and fry the rashers in a non-stick pan in their own fat until crisp. Line a 20 cm/8-inch flan dish with half the bacon. Mix the leeks, spinach, mustard and cress, watercress and herbs and pile them on top of the bacon. Beat two of the eggs, add the stock, season lightly with salt and pepper and pour over the vegetables. Put the remaining bacon over the vegetables. Roll out the pastry and cover the pie, using the trimmings to decorate the top. Beat the remaining egg and brush the pastry generously with it. Bake the pie in a moderate oven (180°C/350°F/Gas Mark 4) for 40 minutes. Serve warm, not hot.

A swiss rabbit with apple

Serves 1
Broadcast
1 January 1985

A nice easy lunch dish which will tax neither your strength nor your hangover after a good New Year's Eve party . . .

18

4 slices of a tart eating
apple, peeled

15 g/½ oz butter or
low-fat margarine

1 slice wholewheat toast

a little dribble of cider

2–4 slices Emmenthal,
Gruyère, Jarlsberg or
cooking Cheddar
cheese, sliced thinly

freshly ground black
pepper

Fry the apple slices lightly in the butter or low-fat margarine. Dribble a little cider over the piece of toast and cover it with half the cheese. Put it under a hot grill until the cheese starts to melt. Put the apple slices on top and cover them with the remains of the cheese. Put it back under the grill until the cheese is melted and lightly browned. Sprinkle over a little black pepper and eat at once.

Tomatoes stuffed with pasta and cod's roe

Serves 4
Broadcast 16 June 1984

Large beef tomatoes are now fairly easy to obtain and give a distinctly mediterranean feel to the dish – even if you are eating it on a cold, wet June day in London. If you are using the really large beef tomatoes you may find that half a tomato will be quite enough for each person.

4 large tomatoes, halved
horizontally with the
middles removed and
reserved

25 g/1 oz butter or
low-fat margarine

2 tablespoons olive or
vegetable oil

1 large onion, peeled
and chopped

2 cloves of garlic, peeled
and chopped finely

a large handful of
chopped parsley

200 g/7 oz can of
pressed cod's roe, diced

50–75 g/2–3 oz cooked
wholewheat tagliatelle,
chopped fairly small

lemon juice

salt and pepper

Put a little butter or margarine in the bottom of each half-tomato and just soften them under a hot grill – they should not cook for more than a couple of minutes if they are not to go soggy.

Meanwhile, heat the oil in a shallow pan and cook the onion and garlic until they are soft and lightly browned. Add the chopped parsley, cod's roe and tagliatelle and mix well. Then add the chopped flesh of the tomatoes and season to taste with the lemon juice, salt and pepper.

Pile the filling into the half-tomatoes, and serve

Wholewheat sesame pasta with Gorgonzola sauce

Serves 6
Broadcast
13 December 1984

This recipe was devised to use the fancy automatic pasta making machine that I had been given as an advance Christmas present! However, even if you are not able to make your own, you can now buy excellent fresh pasta, both plain and wholewheat, quite easily. The sauce is delicious but very rich – you are warned!

450 g/1 lb wholewheat flour

50 g/2 oz sesame seeds, preferably toasted

4 eggs

or

700 g/1½ lbs fresh wholewheat pasta

450 ml/1¾ pint double cream

225 g/8 oz Gorgonzola or dolcelatte cheese, chopped

50 g/2 oz butter or low-fat margarine

juice of 1 large or 2 small oranges

about 75 g/3 oz freshly ground parmesan cheese

salt and freshly ground black pepper

Mix the flour, sesame seeds and eggs together well, either in a bowl or in a pasta making machine. Churn or knead until they are well amalgamated and then feed through the machine to make whatever shape you want. Leave the pasta to dry for 30–45 minutes before using it. You can also use any shape of bought pasta. Cook the pasta in plenty of fast boiling water for 3–4 minutes; keep testing to make sure it does not overcook. Drain and keep it warm.

To make the sauce, put the cream in a saucepan and heat it gently. Add the Gorgonzola or dolcelatte cheese and the butter or margarine. Cook them together gently, stirring continually until both are melted. Add the orange juice, with salt and pepper to taste.

Serve the pasta with plenty of sauce, sprinkled with the parmesan and some more freshly ground black pepper. A salad of watercress and tomatoes goes well with this dish.

'Buttered eggs with anchoves'

Serves 6
Broadcast
29 September 1984

This recipe comes from 'Pepys at Table' which I wrote with Christopher Driver and which was published in October 1984. It included extracts from Samuel Pepys' diaries, seventeenth century recipes that his wife might have used and modern updates of those recipes. The 'buttered eggs with anchoves' comes from the Family Dictionary of 1695 and is delicious as a starter or light lunch dish.

6 large anchovy fillets

3 tablespoons white wine

12 eggs

40 g/1½ oz pistachio nuts, shelled and chopped finely

4 tablespoons good, brown juice from a roast or casserole

25 g/1 oz butter or low-fat margarine

6 slices of wholemeal bread, toasted

freshly ground black pepper

Mash the anchovies in the white wine. Lightly whisk the eggs in a bowl, then add the anchovies and wine, the nuts and the meat juices. Melt the butter or margarine in a pan, add the egg mixture and cook gently as you would scrambled eggs. Serve the eggs either on or with freshly toasted wholemeal bread, with a little freshly ground black pepper.

Baked avocados with fennel

Serves 4
Broadcast
15 March 1984

If you have some bullet-hard avocados which a month in the airing cupboard is not going to improve, this is a good way to deal with them.

15 g/½ oz butter or low-fat margarine

2 rashers of bacon, diced small

1 small onion, chopped very finely

100 g/4 oz fennel, chopped very finely

100 g/4 oz Lancashire, Cheshire or Double Gloucester cheese, crumbled

150 ml/5 fl oz double cream

2 large avocados

salt and pepper

Melt the butter or margarine in a pan and very gently cook the bacon, onion and fennel until they are soft but not browned. Add the cheese and cream and continue to heat gently until the cheese is melted. Season to taste; if the bacon was salty you may not need very much.

Halve the avocados and remove the stones. If the hole in the middle is very small, hollow it out a little more. Put the avocados in an ovenproof dish and fill the middles with the mixture which will probably run over the sides a bit. Bake them in a moderate oven (180°C/350°F/Gas Mark 4) for 20 minutes and eat at once.

Leek and tomato flan

Serves 4
Broadcast
26 April 1984

A combination of leeks and tomatoes makes an excellent salad, but if you want to upgrade it into something a bit more substantial you can turn it into a flan.

175 g/6 oz wholewheat flour

50 g/2 oz butter or low-fat margarine

50 g/2 oz lard or vegetable shortening

8 medium-size leeks, cleaned and sliced thickly

4 large or 8 medium-size tomatoes, skinned

juice of ½ lemon

100 g/4 oz white Stilton, Lancashire, Wensleydale or other crumbly white cheese (optional)

sea salt and freshly ground black pepper

Rub the fats into the flour and make into a firm paste by adding cold water. Roll out the dough, line a 15–18 cm/6–7-inch flan dish and bake it blind (weighting the middle with some foil and some beans or rice) in a moderately hot oven (190°C/ 375°F/Gas Mark 5) for 25 minutes or until it is cooked through. You should remove the foil and beans for the last 5–10 minutes to make sure the base is cooked and not soggy.

Meanwhile, blanch the leeks by cooking them for 2–3 minutes in boiling water – the rawness should be just taken off them but they should remain slightly crisp. Cut the tomatoes into 6, remove the stems and pips and mix them with the leeks. Season lightly with the salt, pepper and lemon juice. Spread the vegetable mixture in the bottom of the flan and return to the oven briefly just to warm the vegetables through, then serve.

Alternatively, sprinkle the crumbled cheese on top of the vegetables and put the flan under a moderately hot grill just to melt the cheese and colour it slightly; serve at once.

Spinach toasts

Serves 6
Broadcast
16 March 1985

The spinach or 'spinnedge' toasts come from a book called Royal Cookery by Patrick Lamb, 'Clerk of the Kitchin' to King Charles II, James II, William and Mary *and* Queen Anne. It was published in 1701 and is filled with the most delicious and (sometimes at least…) quite simple recipes.

675 g/1½ lb fresh or 225 g/8 oz frozen leaf spinach

1 digestive biscuit, crushed or 1 tablespoon wholewheat breadcrumbs

1 tablespoon double cream

2 whole eggs

2 hardboiled egg yolks

1 large cooking apple, peeled and chopped finely

25 g/1 oz currants, washed

15 g/½ oz melted butter or low-fat margarine

a pinch each of salt, brown sugar, black pepper and nutmeg

6 slices of wholewheat toast

If the spinach is fresh, wash it, trim it and cook it for 5 minutes in its own water. Drain it and chop it roughly. If it is frozen, defrost it, drain it thoroughly and chop it roughly.

Soak the biscuit or crumbs in the cream. Beat the eggs and mash the hardboiled yolks. Mix the spinach, apple, biscuit and cream, egg and yolks, currants, butter and spices and pile the mixture on to the pieces of toast. Place the toasts in an ovenproof dish and bake in a moderate oven (180°C/350°F/Gas Mark 4) for 20 minutes. Serve at once.

Pepper, pear and anchovy salad

Serves 6
Broadcast
1 November 1984

4 tablespoons good mayonnaise

6–8 fillets of anchovy, chopped small

lemon juice

1 large red and 1 large green pepper, de-seeded and sliced finely

3 medium-size pears, peeled and sliced thinly

half a head of iceberg lettuce

salt and pepper

Put the mayonnaise in a bowl, add the anchovy. Mix well and then season to taste with salt, pepper and lemon juice. Do take care not to over-salt it, as the saltiness of the anchovies will develop in the mayonnaise. The mayonnaise should be of a 'light coating consistency', like double cream; if it is too thick, thin it with a little boiling water.

Add the peppers and pears and toss gently until both fruit and vegetables are well coated with the dressing. Serve on a bed of crisp iceberg lettuce.

A 'spomlette'

Serves 1
Broadcast
24 March 1984

On Saturday mornings we broadcast a series of recipes for people living on their own – although of course the quantities can be multipled if you want to use them for a family. The 'spomlette' seemed to get over the hazards of cooking both omelettes and scrambled eggs by rolling them into one!

10 g/½ oz of butter or low-fat margarine

1 onion, peeled and chopped roughly

1 clove of garlic, peeled and chopped finely (optional)

1 small red or green pepper, de-seeded and chopped

2 rashers of bacon, diced or 2–3 anchovy fillets, chopped

a few mushrooms, chopped (optional)

1 tomato, chopped (optional)

2 eggs

salt and pepper

1–2 slices wholewheat toast

In a frying pan, melt the butter and briskly fry the onion, garlic, peppers and bacon or anchovies. Let them brown lightly but do not allow to burn. Add the mushrooms and tomato, if you are using them, and cook for a couple of minutes. Reduce the heat slightly. Mix the eggs together with a fork in a cup or bowl and season *lightly* with salt and pepper (both the bacon and anchovy are salty so you do not want to overdo it). Tip the egg mixture into the pan, stir around and cook gently for 2–3 minutes (stirring now and then to prevent it sticking) or until the egg is just set – not bullet hard. Spoon the mixture on to a plate, on or with the toast and eat at once.

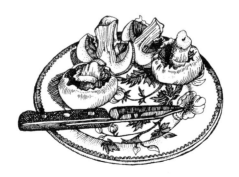

Fish

Salmon, apple and nut salad

Serves 4
Broadcast
27 August 1983

A very easy last-minute salad.

2 large, crisp, tart eating apples

450 g/1 lb fresh cooked salmon or 2 × 205 g/ 7½ oz can of red salmon or 2 × 205 g/7½ oz can of tuna fish

175 g/6 oz cashew nuts

4 tablespoons mayonnaise

about 2 tablespoons lemon juice

a crisp cabbage or iceberg lettuce or 2 bunches of watercress

salt and pepper

Peel the apples if the skin is tough, if not, just core and dice them. Flake the fish and mix it with the apples and nuts. Thin the mayonnaise with the lemon juice and season it to taste with salt and pepper. Toss the fish and apple mixture in the mayonnaise and adjust the seasoning to taste. Arrange the cabbage, lettuce or watercress on a serving dish and pile the fish mixture on the top to serve.

Cod, cream and caper pie

Serves 6
Broadcast
11 October 1984

Now that it has become expensive to buy, cod is being appreciated for the excellent fish that it is. Adding cream to the sauce raises this dish from the everyday to the 'gourmet' level. It freezes well, however, so is practical too, but use only hard-boiled egg yolks in that case.

700 g/1½ lb cod fillets or steaks (fresh if possible)

240 ml/8 fl oz dry white wine

240 ml/8 fl oz water

3 or 4 slices of lemon

65 g/2½ oz butter or low-fat margarine

225 g/8 oz onion, peeled and chopped very finely

40 g/1½ oz flour

150 ml/5 fl oz double cream

3–4 tablespoons capers, drained and chopped roughly

6 hard-boiled eggs

1 kg/2 lb potatoes, peeled

about 150 ml/5 fl oz milk, or milk and cream mixed

salt and white pepper

Poach the fish in the wine and water, with the lemon slices, for about 15 minutes on a hob, or 4–5 minutes in a microwave; do not let it over-cook.

Meanwhile, melt 40 g/1½ oz of the butter and cook the onion until it is quite soft, add the flour, cook for a minute or two, then gradually add the cooking liquid from the fish. Cook together for a couple of minutes, then add the cream and the capers: exactly how many capers you add will depend on how keen you are on capers. Season to taste with salt and pepper. Break the fish into large flakes and gently mix it into the sauce with the hard-boiled eggs, chopped. Spoon the mixture into a pie dish and set aside.

Meanwhile, steam or microwave the potatoes, then mash them with 15 g/½ oz of the butter and as much creamy milk as is needed to make a smooth purée. Season them with salt and pepper.

Spoon the potato carefully over the fish or pipe it on for a really stylish look. Dot the top of the potato with the remaining butter. Reheat the pie in a moderate oven for about 30 minutes at 180°C/350°F/Gas Mark 4 or a microwave. If you use a microwave, you may need to put the pie under a grill for a couple of minutes to brown the top.

Turkish rice and prawn pilaff

Serves 4–6
Broadcast 30 July 1985

This is one of my mother's recipes which has appeared very successfully at every buffet party I can remember since I was a child! It is spicy and interesting, as good cold as hot, and freezes very well.

4 tablespoons olive or sunflower oil

2 small red peppers, de-seeded and chopped finely

1 small onion, peeled and chopped finely

1 clove of garlic, peeled and chopped finely or crushed

4 heaped tablespoons long-grain Patna or brown rice

1/2 teaspoon each ground allspice and cumin seeds

1 heaped teaspoon dried mint or basil

5/6 giant pacific prawns, peeled or 100 g/4 oz ordinary prawns, peeled

2 tablespoons currants, washed

a handful of finely chopped parsley

juice of 1–2 lemons

salt

Heat the oil in a large, flat pan and gently cook the peppers, onion and garlic until they are soft but not browned. Add the rice, spices and herbs, stir around for a few minutes, then add enough water to cover the rice. Bring the mixture to the boil and simmer with the pan uncovered for 10–15 minutes or until the rice is just cooked, but not mushy. You may have to add a little more water if it dries up too fast.

Add the prawns, currants and a generous sprinkling of salt. Cook for a couple more minutes, add the lemon juice and parsley and adjust the seasoning to taste. Serve warm, or cold.

Shellfish couscous

Serves 6
Broadcast
17 January 1985

I found this delicious dish in a Moroccan restaurant in southern Spain. Since couscous is obtainable in most delicatessens, there is no reason why it cannot be done at home.

450 g/1 lb couscous

4 tablespoons olive or corn oil

225 g/8 oz onions, chopped roughly

2 cloves of garlic, chopped finely

1 bulb of fennel, chopped finely

1 teaspoon each turmeric and ground cumin

1 mackerel, cleaned and cut into fairly small pieces

225 g/8 oz tomatoes, chopped roughly

300 ml/½ pint fish stock or water

300 ml/½ pint white wine

900 g/2 lb mussels in their shells, cleaned or 225 g/8 oz frozen mussels

450 g/1 lb clams or cockles in their shells, cleaned or 100 g/4 oz frozen clams or cockles

225–275 g/8–10 oz artichoke hearts, fresh, frozen and thawed or canned and drained

salt and pepper

Follow the cooking instructions for the couscous, moistening it with warm water and then steaming it in a steamer or a colander over a saucepan of boiling water.

In a large pan, heat the oil and gently cook the onions, garlic and fennel with the spices until the vegetables are beginning to soften. Add the mackerel, tomatoes and the liquid. Bring to the boil and as soon as it is boiling briskly add the mussels and clams, bring back to the boil, then add the artichoke hearts (halved or quartered if necessary) and cook the mixture briskly for 4–5 minutes or until the shellfish are all opened and the artichokes heated through. Season to taste with salt and pepper and serve over the couscous.

Arnold Bennett omelette

Serves 6
Broadcast 24 May 1984

It is said that this dish was invented by the chef at the Savoy for Arnold Bennett, the writer, who was addicted to smoked haddock; whether or not this was true, I can see how he could have become addicted to the omelette!

6 eggs

4 tablespoons cold water

350 g/12 oz cooked, smoked haddock, flaked

100 g/4 oz well-flavoured Cheddar cheese, grated

175 ml/6 fl oz double cream

15 g/½ oz butter or low-fat margarine

salt and freshly ground black pepper

Separate the eggs and whisk the yolks in a bowl with a fork. Add the water and some seasoning (do not over-salt as the haddock can be salty) and beat again. Mix in the fish, cheese and half the cream. Whisk the egg whites until they just hold their shape and fold them into the egg yolk mixture. Heat the butter in an omelette pan until it sizzles, pour in the egg mixture and cook over a hot flame as for an omelette. After a couple of minutes when it is half-cooked, pour the rest of the cream over the omelette and put it under a hot grill for 3–4 minutes to finish cooking the eggs and brown the top of the omelette slightly. Sprinkle with freshly ground black pepper and serve at once with plenty of wholemeal bread or toast.

Fettuccine and shrimp salad

If you want a stronger and slightly smokier fish taste, you could substitute two 225 g/8 oz cans of smoked oysters in oil for the potted shrimps.

225 g/8 oz wholewheat fettuccine (or any wholewheat pasta shape)

1 kg/2.2 lb fresh broad beans, shelled

150 g/5 oz can of red pimentos

225 g/8 oz artichoke hearts, freshly cooked, frozen or canned

225 g/8 oz potted shrimps

4 tablespoons olive oil

juice of 3 lemons

sea salt and freshly ground black pepper

a large sprig of fresh basil, chopped or 2 teaspoons dried basil

Cook the pasta in plenty of fast boiling, lightly salted water, making sure that the strands are well separated. At the same time, cook the beans in a little boiling water until they are just cooked but still crunchy. Open and drain the can of pimentos and slice them thinly. Halve or quarter the artichoke hearts.

As soon as the pasta is cooked, drain it well and turn it into a large bowl. While it is still hot, add the beans, pimento, artichoke hearts and shrimps or oysters and mix well. Then add the oil and lemon juice, salt and pepper to taste and mix thoroughly again.

If the pasta looks as though it is going to stick together, add the oil before anything else and stir it in well to separate the strands.

Turn the salad into a serving dish and decorate it with the fresh chopped basil; if you are using dried basil it is better to mix it into the salad with the other ingredients.

Moules à la marinière

Once an 'r' comes back into the month, shellfish such as oysters and mussels suddenly reappear in the fishmongers.

3 kg/6½ lb fresh mussels in their shells

50 g/2 oz butter

Clean the mussels thoroughly, scraping off as many of the barnacles as possible and removing the beard (or byssus) from the

2 large onions, chopped finely

2 cloves of garlic, crushed

300 ml/½ pint dry white wine

1 tablespoon chopped parsley

salt and freshly ground black pepper

extra parsley for garnish, chopped

pointed end. They should all close firmly when tapped; if they do not, throw them out because this means they are dead and *must not be eaten* or they will make you *thoroughly* ill. Heat a large, wide pan and add the butter, onions, crushed garlic, wine, parsley and the mussels. Shake the pan with the lid on and simmer for 5 minutes. If you do not have a large enough pan, split the ingredients into two pans and cook them in two batches.

Take off and discard the empty shell of each mussel. Discard any which do not open. Season the sauce, put the mussels into a hot tureen and spoon over the sauce. If you pour the juices on, the sand which inevitably remains in the mussels goes in too. Sprinkle on the chopped parsley and serve at once.

Leek and tuna pie

Serves 4
Broadcast
3 March 1984

2 × 200 g/7 oz can of tuna fish

a 50 g/2 oz can of anchovies

4 large leeks, washed and sliced finely

350 g/12 oz fresh spinach or 225 g/8 oz frozen leaf spinach, thawed

150 ml/¼ pint dry white wine

450 g/1 lb potatoes, scrubbed and sliced *very* thinly

25 g/1 oz butter or low-fat margarine

Drain the oil from the cans of anchovy and tuna into a shallow pan and gently fry the leeks in this until they are soft but not browned. Turn them into a pie dish. Chop the fresh spinach or drain the frozen spinach and spread it over the leeks. Break up the tuna fish with a fork and chop the anchovies. Mix them thoroughly and spread them over the spinach. Pour over the wine, then cover the pie with the thinly sliced potatoes. Dot the pie with half the butter or margarine, cover it and cook it in a moderate oven (180°C/350°F/Gas Mark 4) for 30 minutes. Take the pie out, dot it with the remaining butter and return it to the oven, uncovered, for a further 15–20 minutes, or until the potatoes are cooked through, and browned on the top. Serve hot.

Fresh salmon cooked in the dishwasher

Broadcast 13 April 1983

No one believed I was serious when I gave out this recipe – but I was, and it really does work! It is fun to do, and the salmon comes out moist and delicious.

1 salmon, cleaned

butter

2 lemons, sliced

1 bulb of fennel, sliced

a handful of fresh chopped parsley

12 peppercorns

Unroll a double length of aluminium foil large enough to make a *very* secure parcel of the salmon. Spread it thickly with the butter and place the salmon on it. Fill the centre of the salmon with lemon slices, fennel and parsley. Spread more butter on the top of the salmon and lay some more lemon and fennel on top. Sprinkle with the peppercorns. Fold the foil very carefully to make a neat parcel of the salmon, double-folding the edges to prevent any water getting in. Place the salmon on the top rack of the dishwasher (you may need to put a flat tray under it if there are spikes on the rack which would pierce the foil). Wash at maximum temperature (65°C on most dishwashers). How long it will take will depend on the size of the salmon; 5–6 lbs takes two full washes. If it is ready before you want to eat it leave it wrapped in the machine where the heat of the dry cycle will keep it warm. When ready to serve, unwrap the parcel and you will find that the salmon has remained beautifully moist and is a marvellous colour. Serve as usual with a butter or Hollandaise sauce.

Creole jambalaya

Serves 4
Broadcast 17 May 1984

Pictured on the front cover.

2 tablespoons lard or bacon fat

2 medium-size green peppers, de-seeded and chopped or roughly sliced

6 large spring onions, cleaned and chopped

2 large onions, peeled and sliced

350 g/12 oz brown rice

175 g/6 oz cooked ham, diced

175 g/6 oz spicy smoked sausage or good pork sausage, diced and lightly fried in its own fat

2 × 400 g/14 oz can of tomatoes, chopped roughly

2 tablespoons tomato purée

225 g/8 oz peeled prawns, cooked or 2 peeled king prawns per person, cooked

salt and pepper

Melt the lard or bacon fat in a large, heavy pan and lightly fry the peppers, spring onions and onions until they begin to brown and crisp up at the edges. Meanwhile, cook the rice in plenty of fast-boiling water for approximately 10–13 minutes or until it is just cooked; drain it thoroughly. Add the rice, ham and diced sausage to the onion and peppers. Then add the tomatoes with their juice and the tomato purée. Stir the mixture well and cook it gently for 30–45 minutes, by which time all the extra juice should be absorbed. Add the prawns 5 minutes before the end. Season with salt and pepper (you may not need much if the ham and sausage are salty) and serve warm.

Meat and poultry

Steak and kidney pie

Serves 6
Broadcast
29 December 1984

A real old favourite, especially with my Colonel friend – regular listeners will remember his marmalade which appears on page 83. Mind you, he likes this cold, and I have to admit that it is also delicious that way.

675 g/1½ lb stewing steak

2–3 tablespoons well-seasoned flour

450 g/1 lb ox or pig's kidney (not lamb's as the flavour is too delicate)

350 g/12 oz button or flat mushrooms

cold water

Trim the steak and cut it into 2-inch cubes. Toss it in the seasoned flour. Trim the kidney, cutting out all the middle, cut it into cubes and toss it in the flour. Remove the stems from the mushrooms (save them for soup), wipe and halve or quarter the tops if necessary and mix them with the meat. Put the whole lot into a pie dish, sprinkle over the rest of the flour and two thirds fill the dish with cold water. Cover it with foil or a lid and cook it in a fairly low

225 g/8 oz wholemeal shortcrust pastry (see page 77)

1 egg, beaten

oven (170°C/325°F/Gas Mark 3) for about 1 hour or until the steak is tender. Take it out of the oven half-way through the cooking and stir around to make sure the flour is well mixed in.

When cooked, top the pie with the pastry (supporting the middle if the dish is rather large for the filling), decorate the top with the pastry trimmings and brush with the beaten egg. Cook in a moderately hot oven (190°C/375°F/Gas Mark 5) for 25–30 minutes or until the crust is cooked and lightly browned. The pie can be eaten hot with vegetables or cold with baked potatoes and a salad. It can be frozen in its dish, topped with pastry, either cooked or uncooked; take care not to burn the pastry in reheating it by covering it with foil if necessary.

Joan Cromwell's 'salat of cold hen'

Serves 6
Broadcast 16 June 1983

Joan was Oliver Cromwell's wife, and it may surprise you to know she wrote an excellent cookery book; this is only one of many recipes which have proved tremendous modern successes.

about 675 g/1½ lb cooked chicken, cut up

the grated rind and juice of 2 large or 3 small lemons

1 tart eating apple, diced

1 small onion, peeled and chopped very finely

2 large handfuls of roughly chopped parsley

3 tablespoons olive oil

sea salt and freshly ground black pepper

In a bowl, mix the chicken, lemon rind, apple, onion and parsley. Sprinkle with sea salt and freshly ground black pepper; then add the lemon juice and olive oil. Mix it well together.

Joan would have served the salad 'garnished with the blanched bones of the hen'. If you want to follow her example, boil the more attractive chicken bones in water with some lemon rind and juice for about ten minutes to whiten them and remove any extra flesh, then use them for garnish.

Broiled collops or chops of pork

Serves 4
Broadcast
20 December 1984

This dish is based on a seventeenth century recipe I discovered when I was researching ideas for my book on Samuel Pepys' cookery.

4 teaspoons each chopped fresh thyme and sage or 2 teaspoons each dried thyme and sage

2 teaspoons sea salt

1 teaspoon freshly ground black pepper

half a small leg of pork, weighing about 1.3–1.5 kg/3–3½ lb, sliced into thick 'collops' or chops or 4 thick pork chops

50 g/2 oz butter or low-fat margarine

25 g/1 oz dark brown sugar

2 tablespoons white wine or cider vinegar

2 tablespoons wholegrain mustard

300 ml/½ pint chicken or veal stock

Mix the herbs, salt and pepper well together. Coat the meat thoroughly in the mixture on both sides, then broil the meat briskly for a couple of minutes on each side in a hot frying pan or under a very hot grill until the outside is crisp. Meanwhile, melt the butter or margarine and sugar in a heavy pan, then add the vinegar and mustard. Mix well, then add the stock; cook together for a minute or two, then add the pork. Cover and simmer for 20–25 minutes. Adjust the seasoning to taste and serve with baked or mashed potatoes.

Chilli exotica

Serves 8
Broadcast
12 April 1984

When working on a little book on peppers, I found all kinds of delicious recipes for Chilli con Carne – in which of course the chilli pepper is an essential ingredient. This is one of the more exotic!

100 g/4 oz dried pinto beans

3 tablespoons lard or low-fat margarine

1 medium-size onion, chopped coarsely

350 g/12 oz spicy pork sausage, chopped

450 g/1 lb lean beef, minced coarsely

4 cloves of garlic, peeled and crushed

1 teaspoon anise or aniseeds

1/2 teaspoon each fennel seeds, ground cloves and cinnamon

1 teaspoon each black and paprika pepper, ground nutmeg and cumin

2 teaspoons dried oregano (Mexican if possible)

4 tablespoons sesame seeds

100 g/4 oz ground almonds

3 whole dried chillies, crushed and soaked in hot water to soften

40 g/1½ oz milk chocolate

175 g/6 oz can tomato purée

3 tablespoons red wine vinegar

1 avocado

salt

Rinse the beans and soak them overnight in 1.2 litres/2 pints of water. Pour them with the water into a heavy pan, add a further pint of water, bring it all to the boil and simmer for 45 minutes uncovered until the beans are partially cooked but still firm. Drain them and reserve the liquid.

Melt 2 tablespoons of the lard or margarine in a heavy pan and fry the beans lightly. Melt the rest of the lard in another pan, add the onion and cook it until soft. In a bowl, combine the sausage and beef with the garlic, herbs and spices. Add this mixture to the onions, breaking up any lumps with a fork. Fry it briskly until the meat is well browned.

Add the reserved liquid to the pot and all the remaining ingredients except the beans and the avocado.

Bring to the boil and simmer, uncovered, for 30 minutes, stirring occasionally. Add a little more water if the mixture looks too dry; it should have the consistency of chunky soup. Add the beans and cook for a further 30 minutes.

Just before serving, adjust the seasoning to taste. Peel and slice the avocado, lightly mix it into the chilli and serve at once.

Bacon, apple and sausagemeat flan

Serves 6
Broadcast
12 November 1983

A real old Catercall favourite which we have served successfully at buffet suppers, cocktail parties, picnics and every other kind of party; it freezes excellently as well.

225 g/8 oz bacon, chopped roughly

1 medium-size onion, chopped roughly and 1 small onion, sliced in rings

100 g/4 oz sausagemeat

1 small cooking apple or a large, tart eating apple

25 g/1 oz rolled or porridge oats

a generous pinch of dried or fresh thyme

175 g/6 oz plain or wholewheat shortcrust pastry (see page 77)

25 g/1 oz butter, melted

salt and pepper

Fry the bacon with the chopped onion in a pan for around 5 minutes or until the bacon is beginning to soften and colour slightly. Work in the sausage meat and continue to cook for a further 5 minutes. Add half the apple, chopped fairly small, with the oats and seasoning.

Line a 20 cm/8-inch flan case with the pastry, spoon the sausage mixture into the middle and even it out. Slice the rest of the apple and lay it over the flan along with the onion rings. Brush them all well with the melted butter. Bake the flan in a moderately hot oven (190°C/375°F/Gas Mark 5) for 40–45 minutes. If the apple and onion look like burning, brush them with a little more butter and cover the flan with a piece of foil or greaseproof paper. Serve the flan warm or cold.

Ham and apple pie

Serves 4
Broadcast 7 May 1983

This recipe is based on a Devon Fidget Pie and is a lovely way to use up a joint of ham which you are getting bored with. You can use sweet potatoes, turnips or celeriac if parsnips are not available.

25 g/1 oz butter or low-fat margarine

225 g/8 oz onions, peeled and sliced roughly

225 g/8 oz parsnips

Melt the butter or margarine in a pan and fry the onion and parsnip until they are lightly coloured but not burnt. Put a layer of this mixture in the bottom of a 20 cm/8-inch pie dish. Cover with half the ham and then the apple. Sprinkle with salt,

450 g/1 lb cooked ham, diced fairly large

225 g/8 oz cooking apples, peeled and sliced

15 g/½ oz dark brown sugar

150 ml/¼ pint cider

225 g/8 oz wholemeal shortcrust pastry (see page 77)

1 egg, beaten

salt and pepper

pepper and sugar. Cover the apple with the rest of the ham and the ham with the rest of the onion mixture; pour in the cider. Top the pie with the pastry, decorate with the trimmings and brush with the beaten egg.

Cook in a moderate oven (180°C/350°F/ Gas Mark 4) for 25–30 minutes or until the pastry is cooked and lightly browned. The pie can be served hot or cold.

Bobotie

Serves 6
Broadcast
6 October 1983

Bobotie is a South African dish whose unexpected ingredients make it the most delicious cross between a pie and a quiche, and a third cousin to a moussaka!

2 slices of thick wholemeal bread

600 ml/1 pint milk

450 g/1 lb cooked lamb

50 g/2 oz butter or low-fat margarine

2 onions, chopped finely

3 tablespoons mild curry powder

juice of 3 lemons

2 teaspoons dark brown sugar

3 eggs

100 g/4 oz toasted, nibbed almonds

100 g/4 oz raisins

salt and pepper

Soak the bread in half the milk for a couple of minutes, then mince it roughly with the cooked lamb in a mincer or food processor. Melt half the butter in a pan and lightly fry the onions with the curry powder. Mix the lemon juice, sugar, salt, pepper and 1 egg in a bowl. Add the onion mixture, then the bread and meat and mix them all well together. Spoon them into an ovenproof dish; if the Bobotie is to be frozen, line the dish with foil. Mix the remaining eggs and milk with the almonds and raisins and pour this over the meat mixture, allowing the liquid to soak well in and making sure that the fruit and nuts are spread out well over the top. Dot with the remaining butter and bake, uncovered, in a moderate oven (180°C/350°F/Gas Mark 4) for 30 minutes or until the top is lightly browned and puffed up. Serve with lots of boiled rice and home-made chutney – although the Bobotie has so much flavour that it scarcely needs the chutney. It is also good cold.

John Nott's sausages

Serves 4
Broadcast
23 February 1984

This recipe comes from a wonderful compendium of dishes published in 1726 by a certain John Nott. The sausages are delicious and do not need to be put in skins, unless you are feeling very energetic.

450 g/1 lb pork belly, skinned and boned with the bones reserved

1 large onion or 4 shallots, peeled and chopped

2 teaspoons sea salt, plus a little extra

½ teaspoon ground mace, plus a little extra

1 teaspoon ground black pepper, plus a little extra

50 g/2 oz fresh spinach

2 teaspoons chopped fresh sage, or sage and savory mixed or 1 teaspoon dried mixed sage and savory

1 teaspoon ground cloves

2 egg yolks

wholemeal flour or breadcrumbs

50 g/2 oz butter or low-fat margarine

Put the pork bones with the onion or shallots and a pinch of salt, pepper and mace in a small saucepan with water just to cover them. Bring them to the boil and simmer them for 30 minutes removing any scum as it rises. Meanwhile, mince the pork with the spinach, herbs and spices. Add the egg yolks, then about 4 tablespoons of the stock from the bones – you need just enough to make the mixture reasonably moist.

If you have a sausage skinning machine (or can persuade your butcher to do it for you) the mixture can now be fed into skins. If you decide to do without skins, form the mixture into sausage shapes and roll them lightly in the flour or breadcrumbs. Fry them gently in the butter or margarine on all sides until cooked through and lightly browned all over. Serve them hot or cold with pickles or mustard – although they have so much flavour of their own they scarcely need anything else!

Irish stew

Serves 4
Broadcast
17 March 1983

It being my first St Patrick's day on the programme, we simply had to have Irish stew. Many people think that Irish stew should be 'tarted up' by adding lots of exotica to it, but in fact the essence of the whole thing is to keep it simple.

675 g/1½ lb potatoes, scrubbed or peeled and sliced thickly

450 g/1 lb scrag end of lamb

100 g/4 oz onions, peeled and sliced thickly

1.2 litres/2 pints cold water

salt and pepper

Put half the sliced potatoes in the bottom of a large saucepan. Remove any large lumps of fat from the meat and put it over the potatoes. Cover the meat with the onions, and the onions with the rest of the potatoes. Season the pot well with salt and pepper and add the water.

Bring the pot rapidly to the boil, skimming off any scum that rises. Turn down the heat and let it cook *very* gently for 2–3 hours or until the meat is falling off the bone. Remove the pot from the heat and let it cool completely, overnight in the fridge if possible. Remove any extra fat which has formed on the top.

To serve, re-heat the stew and adjust the seasoning to taste. There should be enough juice for you to have a plate of 'soup' first and then the stew proper.

Pot roast

Serves 4
Broadcast
7 January 1984

This is such an easy dish to do that it should be on every ham-fisted cook's list of favourites, and it tastes delicious, particularly on a cold winter's night.

15 g/½ oz butter or low-fat margarine

675 g/1½ lb topside or well-trimmed brisket, rolled and tied

about 450 g/1 lb onions, peeled and sliced roughly

a bottle of red wine

100 g/4 oz black olives (optional)

salt and pepper

In a flameproof casserole (one not much bigger than the piece of meat if possible) melt the butter and brown the meat over a high heat. Add the onions and then red wine until the meat is completely covered. Add a little salt and pepper. Cover tightly and cook in a slow oven (150°C/300°F/Gas Mark 2) or on a very low heat for 2 hours or until the beef is really tender when you stick a knife in it. Add the olives if you like the flavour and return to the oven for another half-hour. Adjust the seasoning to taste and serve surrounded with the onions and juices and accompanied by baked potatoes.

Braised rolls of beef

Serves 4–6
Broadcast
27 February 1985

This is another of the Colonel's favourites! I invented it especially for my freezer book, so bear in mind that it might be worth doing more than you need and freezing some for future use.

450 g/1 lb lean braising beef or rump steak, sliced horizontally in thin strips

175 g/6 oz freshly minced pork

a generous pinch each of marjoram and oregano

¼ teaspoon allspice

4 tablespoons medium-dry sherry

350 g/12 oz mushrooms

4–6 rashers of back bacon

50 g/2 oz butter or low-fat margarine

2 tablespoons oil

300 ml/½ pint red wine

300 ml/½ pint good beef stock or consommé

1 level tablespoon flour

a handful of chopped parsley

salt and freshly ground black pepper

Flatten the strips of beef and sprinkle them with salt and pepper. Mix the pork with the herbs, allspice and sherry and spread it over the beef strips. Slice about 100 g/4 oz of the mushrooms finely and lay them down the middle of each strip. Roll up the strip carefully, lengthways, trying to keep as much of the filling inside as possible. Then roll each beef roll in a rasher of bacon and secure it with string or a cocktail stick.

Melt half the fat and oil in a heavy-based pan and briskly fry the rolls until they are tanned all over. Add the wine and stock, cover the pan and simmer gently for one hour. Alternatively, the beef can be cooked in a moderate oven (180°C/350°F/Gas Mark 4) for the same amount of time.

When the beef is cooked, slice the remaining mushrooms finely. Cook them lightly in the rest of the butter and oil. Add the flour, stir and cook for a couple of minutes, then gradually add the strained juices from the pan to make the sauce. Adjust the seasoning if necessary. Remove the rolls, slice them neatly so that the different layers are visible, and put them on a warmed serving dish. Spoon the mushrooms over the slices, pour over the sauce and sprinkle with the parsley. Serve with new potatoes and a green vegetable.

Sir Kenelm Digby's stewed beef with cheese

Serves 6
Broadcast
10 November 1983

Sir Kenelm was 'Master of the Queen's Wardrobe' to Charles I's wife, and a keen gourmet. None of his recipes were published during his lifetime as he did not regard cookery as a suitable occupation for a gentleman. However, his son had no such qualms. His 'stewed beef' sounds strange but is actually delicious.

300 g/11 oz white cabbage, sliced finely

1 large onion, peeled and sliced finely

50 g/2 oz beef suet, chopped

½ teaspoon each ground mace, nutmeg and black pepper

1 teaspoon salt

1 teaspoon dried sage

2 teaspoons dried thyme

1 bay leaf

150 g/5 oz strong Cheddar cheese, grated

90 ml/3 fl oz red wine vinegar

300 ml/½ pint red wine

675 g/1½ lb stewing beef, trimmed and cubed

Mix the cabbage and onion and place half of this in an ovenproof casserole or pot. In a bowl, mix the suet, spices, salt, herbs and cheese, add the wine and vinegar and then the beef. Mix them well and turn them into the casserole. Top with the rest of the cabbage and onion, cover tightly and bake in a moderate oven (170°C/325°F/Gas Mark 3) for 1½–2 hours or until the beef is really tender. Serve from the pot.

Gigot d'agneau aux groseilles et cressons

Serves 6–8
Broadcast
11 August 1984

This is also delicious cold – which is useful as there seems to be a dearth of interesting things to do with cold lamb! If fresh or frozen redcurrants are not available, you could use cranberries.

1 leg of lamb weighing about 2 kg/4½ lb

a large sprig of rosemary

2 bunches of watercress

225 g/8 oz redcurrants

1 tablespoon redcurrant jelly

4 tablespoons sweet white wine

Roast the lamb as usual for about 20 minutes for every 450 g/1 lb, resting it on the sprig of rosemary.

Meanwhile, cook the watercress and fruit together, either in a pan or a microwave; you will not need to add any more liquid than is already in them. Add the redcurrant jelly and the wine, cook for a minute or two more just to melt the jelly and then put the mixture into a food processor or liquidiser. Once puréed, put it through a sieve to remove the pips, then set aside until the lamb is cooked.

Remove the lamb from the oven and very carefully skim the fat from the top of the juices; add the juices to the sauce. Mix them well together and taste for seasoning; you may need a little more salt or pepper, although I found that neither was really necessary. Serve the lamb with the sauce, a little spooned over each portion.

To serve the lamb cold: proceed as above but do not add the juices to the sauce as soon as it is cooked. Drain them off and let them cool entirely so that you can remove all the fat. When you are absolutely sure there is no fat left, add the juices, which may have jellied slightly, to the sauce. If they have jellied, heat the whole thing gently until they melt and then amalgamate them well. Slice the lamb very thinly and put it on a platter, then spoon the sauce (which should be quite thick because of the jellied juices) over the top. The dish tastes even better and looks particularly pretty if you serve it with some cold French beans which have been *very* lightly cooked and allowed to get cold. You can arrange them in a circle or fan shape on the dish with the lamb in the middle.

Capon or turkey roast in honey

Serves 8–10
Broadcast
31 March 1984

This is a lovely way to cook a special occasion bird, as the honey makes the skin dark and shiny and the flesh remains dazzlingly white.

1 capon or small turkey weighing about 3.5–4.5 kg/8–10 lb, with giblets

75 g/3 oz butter or low-fat margarine

1 medium-size onion, chopped finely

a large handful of finely chopped parsley

1 tart eating apple or half a cooking apple, peeled and chopped small

75 g/3 oz plump raisins

grated rind and juice of 1½ lemons

75 g/3 oz ground almonds

75 g/3 oz wholemeal breadcrumbs

1 teaspoon ground ginger

1 teaspoon salt

½ teaspoon black pepper

1 egg

2 tablespoons honey

Remove the giblets from the bird, keep the liver and chop it; throw out the rest. Melt 25 g/1 oz of the butter in a saucepan and gently cook the liver, onion and parsley until the liver is firm and the onion soft. Take the pan off the heat and add the apple, raisins, lemon rind and juice, almonds, breadcrumbs, seasonings and egg. Mix the whole lot together well and use it to stuff the bird at both ends. Secure it with skewers and put it in a roasting pan. Melt the remaining butter and honey together and spoon them over the bird; as it cools it will cling to the skin. Leave the bird to marinate in the honey, uncovered, in a fridge or larder, for 24 hours, spooning over any excess marinade from time to time.

Roast the bird in a moderate oven (180°C/ 350°F/Gas Mark 4), basting frequently with the honey and butter mixture, for 20 minutes per pound. The skin will gradually turn black and shiny, in sharp contrast to the white meat below. Serve hot or cold.

Aubergine and sausage casserole

Serves 6
Broadcast
30 March 1985

A tasty and filling casserole which I found in America; it freezes excellently.

6–8 tablespoons olive or sunflower oil

2 medium-size aubergines, sliced thickly lengthways

15 g/½ oz butter or low-fat margarine

450 g/1 lb good quality sausagemeat

half a bunch of spring onions, cleaned and chopped

225 g/8 oz mushrooms, chopped roughly

1 tablespoon wholegrain or french mustard

1 tablespoon Worcestershire sauce

150 ml/¼ pint red wine

salt and pepper

225–350 g/8–12 oz tomatoes, sliced

50 g/2 oz well-flavoured Cheddar cheese, grated

50 g/2 oz wholemeal breadcrumbs

Heat the oil in a heavy-bottomed pan and fry the aubergines until they are lightly tanned on each side. In a separate pan, melt the butter and briskly fry the sausage-meat until it begins to colour. Add the chopped spring onions and mushrooms and cook all together for a couple of minutes. Add the mustard and Worcester-shire sauce and wine and a little salt and pepper.

Put half the aubergines in the bottom of an ovenproof dish (lined with foil if you intend to freeze it), cover them with the sausage mixture, then with a second layer of the aubergines. Cover the aubergines with the sliced tomatoes. Mix together the cheese and breadcrumbs and sprinkle them over the top of the tomatoes.

Bake the casserole in a moderate oven (180°C/350°F/Gas Mark 4) for 30 minutes or until the top is well browned. Serve at once.

Marinade for barbecued beef

Serves 6
Broadcast
16 July 1984

A sunny July brings all the barbecues out into the garden, so it is as well to be prepared with good marinade recipes; this one comes from the United States.

2 large cloves of garlic

6 spring onions

4 tablespoons olive or vegetable oil

2 tablespoons soya sauce

3 tablespoons honey

2 tablespoons vinegar

2 teaspoons ground ginger

6 rump or fillet steaks, or 18 pork spare-ribs

Peel and finely chop the garlic and spring onions. Mix all the ingredients for the marinade together well and put them in a dish. Put in the steaks or ribs and make sure they are submerged in the marinade. Leave for at least four hours and preferably about 12 before barbecuing as normal. Use the remains of the marinade to baste the meat as it cooks.

Pineapple chicken

Serves 4
Broadcast
26 November 1983

This recipe originally came from a diet sheet, but it is so easy and so good that it has moved into my standard repertoire.

1 chicken weighing about 1.5 kg/3½ lb, jointed

1 large onion, sliced thinly into rings

1 teaspoon rosemary leaves

1 teaspoon sea salt

½ teaspoon ground ginger

420 ml/14 fl oz can of unsweetened pineapple juice

a pinch each of black pepper and paprika

Arrange the chicken joints in an ovenproof dish, arrange the onion rings on them and add all the seasonings. Pour over the pineapple juice and put the dish, uncovered, in a moderate oven (180°C/350°F/Gas Mark 4). Bake it for approximately 45 minutes or until the chicken is cooked and brown on the top.

47

Banger and bean pot

Serves 4–6
Broadcast
18 February 1984

A really filling, warming February dish.

450 g/1 lb mixed dried beans (pinto or kidney beans will need to be soaked and boiled for 15 minutes first)

4 fat rashers of bacon, chopped

2 onions, peeled and chopped roughly

15 g/½ oz root ginger, peeled and sliced thinly (optional)

1 large clove of garlic, peeled and chopped finely (optional)

about 225 g/8 oz carrots, scrubbed and diced roughly

about 225 g/8 oz parsnips, scrubbed and diced roughly

8 good quality frankfurters, sliced thickly

1 tablespoon mixed dried herbs or 2 tablespoons of fresh mixed herbs

600 ml/1 pint red wine

600 ml/1 pint water

1 teaspoon black peppercorns, or freshly ground black pepper

sea salt

Soak and parcook any beans which need it.

In a large casserole, fry the bacon, then add the onions, root ginger, garlic, carrots, and parsnips and cook in the bacon fat until they are well browned. Add the frankfurters and the herbs and fry for a minute or two more. Then add the beans, liquid and the peppercorns or pepper, bring to the boil and simmer for 1½–2 hours or until the beans are well cooked. Season to taste with sea salt and serve.

The bean pot will be even better if you can cook it a couple of days before you want to eat it so that the flavours have time to develop.

Vegetables, vegetarian dishes and salads

Fennel and strawberry salad

Serves 6
Broadcast
11 April 1985

This is delicious as a light starter or as a rather classy side salad.

3 small bulbs of fennel

3 tablespoons natural yogurt, preferably a fairly creamy one

juice of 1–1½ lemons

about 12 mint leaves, fresh if possible

about 20 strawberries, halved or quartered if large

Trim the fennel, reserving a few nice leaves for garnish and slice it thinly. Blanch the slices in boiling water for 3 minutes, cool under cold water and drain. Meanwhile, mix the yogurt with the lemon juice and mint leaves, adding the latter gradually and tasting as you go, as the flavour is very strong and can swamp the rest. You may want to add a little salt, although I did not find it necessary.

Toss the fennel and the halved or quartered strawberries in the dressing and arrange on a serving dish. Decorate with some fennel leaves.

49

Chilled, stuffed courgettes

Serves 8
Broadcast
16 August 1984

These are a bit of a fiddle to prepare but well worth it; you can use them as a starter or as a rather fancy salad.

8 medium-size courgettes

1 spanish onion, peeled and chopped very finely

1 clove of garlic, peeled and crushed

4–6 tablespoons well-flavoured french dressing

3 tomatoes, peeled, de-seeded and chopped finely

1 green pepper, de-seeded and chopped finely

1 tablespoon finely chopped capers

1 teaspoon each finely chopped parsley and basil, if available

salt and pepper

Simmer the courgettes unpeeled, but topped and tailed, in boiling, salted water until they are half-cooked – a couple of minutes should be enough. Cut them in half lengthways, scoop out the seeds and chop the seeds and flesh. Cover with half the onion, and the garlic and sprinkle with some french dressing. Leave to marinate for a couple of hours.

Mix the remaining onion, tomatoes, pepper, capers, parsley and basil with the chopped courgette flesh. Toss in more of the dressing and fill the courgette shells with the mixture. Arrange on a dish to serve.

Stuffed vegetable marrow

Serves 4
Broadcast 26 July 1984

Marrows have an awful tendency to be both watery and tasteless, so it is best to stuff them with something tasty. Remember to use rice or a pulse as in this recipe, however, rather than breadcrumbs which go soggy as they absorb the marrow juices. Use only a young marrow.

2 tablespoons vegetable oil

2 medium-size onions, peeled and chopped roughly

3 cloves of garlic, peeled and chopped finely

1 green chilli, de-seeded and chopped finely

225 g/8 oz bacon rashers, chopped

6 tablespoons brown rice

4 tomatoes, chopped roughly

150 ml/¼ pint medium-dry sherry

150 ml/¼ pint water

1 young vegetable marrow weighing about 675 g/1½ lb

a handful of chopped parsley

3 tablespoons sunflower seeds

75 g/3 oz wholemeal breadcrumbs or toasted oatmeal (optional)

salt and pepper

Heat the oil in a heavy pan and add the onions, garlic, chilli and bacon. Fry them until they are lightly tanned all over. Add the rice, stir around for a couple of minutes, then add the tomatoes, sherry and water. Bring to the boil and simmer for 10–15 minutes or until the rice is just cooked; if it dries up, add a little more water. Carefully halve the marrow and cut out most of the insides; chop them roughly. Add the chopped marrow to the rice mixture with the parsley, sunflower seeds and seasoning to taste. Put the marrow shells into an ovenproof dish and pile the stuffing mixture into them. Pour a little water or wine into the bottom of the dish, sprinkle them with the breadcrumbs or toasted oatmeal if you want a crisp top and bake them in a moderate oven (180°C/350°F/Gas Mark 4) for 20–30 minutes or until the shells are soft but not soggy. Eat hot or cold.

Parsnips Molly Parkin

Serves 6
Broadcast
10 November 1984

I have had this recipe for as long as I can remember, although I absolutely cannot remember where it came from, which seems unfair since it is so delicious! It also freezes well.

1 kg/2.2 lb parsnips, scrubbed, topped and tailed and sliced thinly

about 5 tablespoons vegetable oil

75 g/3 oz butter or low-fat margarine

675 g/1½ lb tomatoes, peeled and sliced thickly

3 level tablespoons soft brown sugar

175 g/6 oz grated Cheddar or other strong-flavoured hard cheese

450 ml/¾ pint double cream

4 rounded tablespoons fresh wholemeal breadcrumbs

salt and pepper

Heat the oil in a heavy pan and briskly fry the parsnips on both sides until they are lightly browned.

Meanwhile, grease a 1.2-litre/2-pint casserole dish with half the butter or margarine.

Layer the parsnips and tomatoes alternately, sprinkling each layer with salt and pepper, sugar, cheese and cream and ending with a layer of parsnips topped with cream and cheese. Sprinkle the breadcrumbs over the top and bake in a moderate oven (170°C/325°F/Gas Mark 3) for 40 minutes. Serve at once.

Red cabbage and apple casserole

Serves 4
Broadcast
29 October 1983

This is a very north European dish; it conjures up warming visions of German beer cellars in my mind. It can be used as a vegetable or on its own as a supper dish.

2 medium-size onions, peeled and chopped

1 bulb of fennel, chopped roughly

Mix the onions, fennel, cabbage, bacon (if used), apple and caraway seeds in a bowl. Mix the yogurt with the horseradish, season lightly with salt and pepper and

450 g/1 lb red cabbage, sliced fairly thinly

4 rashers of bacon, chopped (optional)

2 large tart eating apples or 1 large cooking apple, peeled and chopped

4 teaspoons caraway seeds

300 ml/½ pint natural yogurt

2 teaspoons horseradish sauce

salt and pepper

mix well into the vegetables. Turn the mixture into an ovenproof casserole, cover tightly and bake in a low oven (150°C/300°F/ Gas Mark 2) for 1½ hours. If possible, take the casserole out and give it a stir once or twice during cooking.

Serve hot, either by itself with lots of fresh rye bread, or as a vegetable with a fairly plain meat dish, such as brisket or silverside.

Stovie pot

Serves 6
Broadcast
20 September 1984

A 'stovie pot' is a traditional Scottish vegetable dish which is quite good enough to be eaten by itself for lunch or supper. It is also excellent with roast pork, boiled gammon or bacon as a side dish, in which case this quantity would be enough for 10 people. If you want a vegetarian dish, you can leave out the bacon and substitute margarine for the dripping or lard – it is still excellent.

50 g/2 oz dripping or lard

450 g/1 lb onions, chopped roughly

12 rashers streaky bacon, chopped roughly

1.5 kg/3½ lb potatoes, unpeeled, scrubbed and sliced thickly

salt and pepper

Melt the dripping or lard until it smokes in a heavy-bottomed pan with a close-fitting lid. Add the onions and bacon, stir around for a couple of minutes, then add a third of the potato slices. Sprinkle them lightly with salt and pepper, add another third, season again, add the rest of the potatoes and a final sprinkling of seasoning. Cover the pot closely, turn the heat down very low and cook for 1½ hours. Take off the lid, stir the contents, re-cover and continue to cook for a further hour or until the potatoes are done. If you already have the oven on, the Stovie Pot can also be cooked in a very low oven, (150°C/300°F/Gas Mark 2).

Vegetable dahl

Serves 4
Broadcast 2 June 1984

2 tablespoons corn or vegetable oil

2 medium-size onions, peeled and sliced finely

1 large clove of garlic, peeled and chopped finely

½ teaspoon ground cumin

¼ teaspoon cayenne pepper

1 medium-size aubergine, diced, with the skin on

100 g/4 oz red lentils

600 ml/1 pint chicken or vegetable stock

1 teaspoon salt

1 teaspoon tomato purée

225 g/8 oz potatoes, scrubbed and diced

1 small cauliflower, broken into florets

1 teaspoon turmeric

2–4 teaspoons garam masala

Heat the oil in a heavy pan and gently fry the onions, garlic, cumin and cayenne for a couple of minutes. Add the aubergine, lentils, stock, salt and tomato purée, cover and simmer for approximately 30 minutes.

Meanwhile put the potatoes and cauliflower in two separate pans, each with a bare 2 cm/1 inch of water in the bottom to which you have added ½ teaspoon of turmeric. Cover them both and simmer until the vegetables are just tender, then drain. When the aubergine mixture is ready, stir in the garam masala to taste and the drained vegetables. Serve with brown rice and popadoms.

'Dirty rice'

Serves 4
Broadcast 9 April 1984

This is a Texan version of Risotto Milanese, and none the worse for that! It is meant to go with barbecued ribs, or any other well-spiced dish.

4 rashers of streaky bacon, chopped

2 small onions, peeled and chopped finely

In a large frying pan, gently cook the bacon in its fat, with the onions. When they are nearly soft, add the livers, mushrooms and corn and cook for a further two minutes.

2 chicken livers, chopped finely

50 g/2 oz mushrooms, chopped finely

3 baby corn (if available) chopped small or 50 g/2 oz sweetcorn

175 g/6 oz unhusked brown rice

450 ml/¾ pint chicken stock

salt and pepper

Add the rice, stir for a couple of minutes, then add the stock. Bring to the boil and cook, boiling fast for 10–15 minutes or until the rice is cooked but not soggy. Do not forget that the unhusked rice will always remain slightly chewy! If the rice dries up before it is cooked, add a little more stock or water. Season to taste and serve hot or warm.

A wholemeal dumpling

Serves 4
Broadcast
17 February 1983

I invented this recipe for a BBC programme which needed a good eighteenth century dumpling to fill the middle of the table and was so enthused by it that I ate the whole of the experimental one myself! Dumplings are a sadly neglected alternative to potatoes or Yorkshire pudding with the Sunday joint.

50 g/2 oz beef suet (fresh is nice but 'packet' is quite acceptable)

50 g/2 oz butter or low-fat margarine

100 g/4 oz wholemeal flour

50 g/2 oz fresh wholemeal breadcrumbs

40 g/1½ oz raisins

grated rind of 1 small lemon

240 ml/8 fl oz milk

about 1 litre/1¾ pints stock

sea salt and freshly ground black pepper

Rub the suet and butter into the flour and breadcrumbs as though you were making pastry. Add the raisins and lemon rind, season with salt and pepper and add the milk. Mix the whole lot together well: it will make a fairly 'wet' mixture. Put the dumpling mixture in the middle of a well-floured cloth – a piece of muslin or a new J cloth will do fine – and tie it securely into a ball. Alternatively, make 4 individual dumplings and tie each separately. Submerge the dumpling in the stock (or into soup or a stock pot if you happen to have one) and simmer it gently for 30–45 minutes, depending on whether you have made individual dumplings or just one. Remove the dumpling, drain it and untie it carefully. Serve it with the joint and lots of good gravy.

Cauliflower cheese with almonds

Serves 4
Broadcast
22 March 1984

1 large cauliflower, broken into florets

2 medium-size onions, peeled and chopped roughly

4 rashers of bacon, chopped

25 g/1 oz butter or low-fat margarine

40 g/1½ oz flour

450 ml/¾ pint milk

175 g/6 oz strong Cheddar or other hard cheese, grated

75 g/3 oz whole almonds

salt and pepper

Steam or microwave the cauliflower florets and onion until they are just cooked but not soggy. Set them aside and keep them warm; reserve the water.

In a pan, lightly fry the bacon in the butter until it is crisp, then add the flour, mix well and cook for a minute or two. Gradually add the milk and a little of the cooking water to make a light white sauce. Add most of the cheese and the almonds, cook for a minute or two, then season to taste; if the bacon was salty you may not need much more salt.

Arrange the cauliflower and onion in a warmed, ovenproof dish, pour over the sauce and sprinkle the remaining cheese on the top. Brown under a hot grill and serve at once.

Stewed cucumbers

Serves 6
Broadcast
8 October 1983

We think of cucumbers only as salad vegetables, but our forefathers were more adventurous and cooked them; they have a delicious flavour when cooked and keep their crispness remarkably well. This recipe comes from my Olde Englishe Recipe Book and is based on a nineteenth century recipe by Dr William Kitchener.

25 g/1 oz butter or low-fat margarine

2 tablespoons olive or vegetable oil

3 medium-size cucumbers, peeled and dried in a cloth, de-seeded and cut into 5 cm/2-inch matchsticks

4 tablespoons wholemeal flour

12 small white onions, peeled

300 ml/½ pint light chicken or veal stock or water and white wine mixed

salt and pepper

Heat the butter and oil in a fairly flat pan. Toss the cucumbers in the flour, then brown them, with the onions, in the butter and oil. When they are lightly tanned all over, add the stock, cover the pan and simmer gently for 15 minutes. With a slotted spoon, remove the cucumbers and onions to a heated serving dish. Reduce the sauce to a thick cream by boiling briskly, adjust the seasoning to taste and pour over the cucumbers and onions. Serve at once.

Watercress, celery and anchovy salad

Serves 6
Broadcast
6 September 1984

3 bunches of watercress

¼–½ cucumber, sliced thinly

3 sticks of celery, chopped finely

4 hard-boiled eggs, chopped roughly

6 medium-size spring onions or a medium-size bunch of chives, chopped

4 tablespoons home-made or good quality bought mayonnaise

1–2 tablespoons lemon juice

about 12 anchovies

First make a bed of watercress on a dish, reserving one sprig for decoration. Arrange the sliced cucumber in a ring on top, leaving a border of watercress round the outside.

Mix the chopped celery, egg and spring onion or chives, then toss them in the mayonnaise which should be thinned to the consistency of double cream, if necessary, with the lemon juice.

Decorate the dish with the anchovies and the reserved watercress.

Soufflé baked potatoes

An easy way to 'tart up' a baked potato. Potato freaks will claim that the cheese merely masks the flavour of the potato, so I have made it optional. Use the following quantities for each person.

1 large baking potato

25 g/1 oz butter or low-fat margarine

25 g/1 oz mushrooms, wiped and chopped roughly

1 egg

salt and black pepper

a little grated nutmeg

25–50 g/1–2 oz grated cheese (optional)

Scrub the potatoes and bake them in a moderate oven (180°C/350°F/Gas Mark 4) until they are soft all through and have nice, crisp skins. Depending on size this can take from 40 minutes to an hour or more; a skewer stuck through the middle will speed the process up. Meanwhile, fry the mushrooms in half the butter.

Take the potatoes out of the oven, split them in half, without cutting through the bottom of the skin and remove about two thirds of the insides. Mash this with the rest of the butter or margarine and season well. Mix the mushrooms into the potato. Separate the eggs and mix the yolks into the potato and mushrooms. Whisk the egg whites until they are just holding their shape in soft peaks and fold them into the mixture. Pile this back into the skins, put them in an ovenproof dish, return them to the oven (which should now be at 180°C/375°F/Gas Mark 5) and bake them for 20 minutes or until the fillings are puffed and browned. Eat at once.

If you are of the cheese-loving brigade, add half the grated cheese to the potatoes along with the mushrooms and pile the rest on top before they go back in the oven.

Desserts

St Valentine's gingered pears

Serves 6
Broadcast
14 February 1985

Tradition has it that both pears and ginger are effective aphrodisiacs, so what could be more suitable for St Valentine's day?

4 ripe pears, peeled and sliced

6 pieces of stem ginger, sliced finely

2 tablespoons ginger syrup from the stem ginger pot

450 ml/¾ pint ginger wine

Lay the pear slices in a shallow pan and sprinkle over the pieces of ginger with their syrup. Pour over the ginger wine. Bring the mixture slowly to the boil and simmer gently for 5 minutes or until the pear slices are cooked. Cool and serve the dish cold – with cream if you like, though I think it masks the flavour.

Rhubarb crumble

Serves 4
Broadcast
12 February 1983

Early, forced rhubarb, which many think has a better flavour than the later, outdoor stuff, is just coming in at the beginning of February, and it makes wonderful crumble! You can use all wholemeal flour to give a slightly 'breadier' topping.

675 g/1½ lb rhubarb, trimmed and wiped

2 tablespoons honey

juice of 1 lemon

75 g/3 oz wholemeal flour

25 g/1 oz white flour

50 g/2 oz dark brown sugar

40 g/1½ oz butter or low-fat margarine

Cut the rhubarb into large chunks and put it, with the honey and the lemon juice, into a double boiler or an ovenproof casserole. Cook it slowly over a low heat, or in a moderate oven, if you happen to have it on, until the rhubarb is soft. This should not take more than 20 minutes. Drain off the juice (drink it for breakfast) and spoon the rhubarb into a pie dish. Rub the flours, sugar and butter or margarine together as if you were making pastry. When it is really well crumbled, sprinkle it in a thick layer over the rhubarb and cook it in a moderate oven (180°C/350°F/Gas Mark 4) for 30 minutes or until the rhubarb is bubbling and the topping crisp. Serve hot or warm with plenty of thick cream or yogurt.

Blackcurrant or raspberry and pear cobbler

Serves 4–6
Broadcast
23 February 1985

You can use frozen blackcurrants or raspberries to make this pudding in mid-winter when pears are in season, and hot, filling puddings go down a bundle.

½ teaspoon cinnamon

¼ teaspoon nutmeg

1 level teaspoon cornflour

150 ml/¼ pint water

225 g/8 oz blackcurrants or raspberries, fresh or frozen

100 g/4 oz brown sugar

Mix the spices and cornflour, then gradually add the water to make a smooth paste. Put the soft fruit and 50 g/2 oz sugar in a pan, add the liquid, bring gradually to the boil and simmer for 3 minutes. Put the peeled and sliced pears in an 20 cm/8-inch pie dish and pour over the blackcurrant or raspberry mixture.

Meanwhile, mix the flour, remaining sugar and baking powder in a bowl. Add

2 large pears, peeled and sliced

150 g/6 oz wholemeal flour

1 teaspoon baking powder

40 g/1½ oz butter, melted

1 egg

150 ml/¼ pint soured cream

the melted butter (slightly cooled), egg and soured cream and mix them thoroughly. Drop spoonfuls of the mix on top of the fruit until it is almost all covered. Bake in a hot oven (190°C/375°F/Gas Mark 5) for 30 minutes or until a skewer comes out of the crust clean. Serve hot with cream.

Cheese and apple pie

Serves 6
Broadcast
29 March 1984

'Apple pie without cheese is like a kiss without a squeeze', or so goes the old Yorkshire saying. This recipe was developed by the Cordon Bleu school, however, to encourage the use of English cheese in cooking. The result is delicious.

150 g/5 oz plain flour

175 g/6 oz butter or low-fat margarine

100 g/4 oz double Gloucester cheese, grated finely

1 egg yolk

1 tablespoon water

1 kg/2.2 lb Cox's Pippins apples

50 g/2 oz butter or low-fat margarine

2–3 tablespoons soft brown sugar

a pinch of cinnamon

grated rind and juice of 1 lemon

Cut, then rub 100 g/4 oz of the butter or margarine into the flour; do not handle it any more than you must or the pastry will be heavy. Add the cheese and stir it in with a knife. Mix the water with the egg yolk, tip it into the flour mixture and mix to a firm dough. Knead for a minute, then chill for at least half an hour.

Meanwhile peel, core and quarter the apples and cut each quarter in half. Fry them lightly in the remaining butter or margarine, dusting them with the sugar. Add the cinnamon and lemon rind, turn into the pie dish and pour over the lemon juice; allow to cool.

Roll out the pastry and cover the pie, lining the rim with a strip of the pastry first and wetting and pressing the edges down well. Brush the pastry lightly with water and dust it with castor sugar. Bake in a moderately hot oven (190°C/375°F/Gas Mark 5) for 20–30 minutes or until the top is cooked and lightly browned. Serve hot or cold, with cream if you like.

Chocolate fruit fondue

Serves 4
Broadcast
24 November 1984

Fruit fondue was all the rage in America recently and although the Swiss Centre assure me that they have been serving sweet fondues for years, no one else in Europe seems to have ever heard of them! It is a very easy and very exotic way to serve fruit for a dinner or a buffet party.

a good selection of firm, fresh fruits (the best are pineapple, watermelon, melon, mandarin orange segments etc.), peeled where necessary and diced

Chocolate sauce:

4 tablespoons drinking chocolate powder

2 tablespoons cocoa powder

2 tablespoons dark brown sugar

300 ml/½ pint water

25 g/1 oz butter or low-fat margarine

Mix the chocolate, cocoa and sugar together, then gradually mix in the water. Heat them gently, then add the butter or margarine. Simmer very gently for 5 minutes, then turn into a fondue dish to keep warm. Alternatively, make the sauce in the fondue dish from the start. Put the sauce in the middle of a platter over a low heat, surrounded with mounds of the fresh fruit pieces which should be small enough to pierce with a fork, fondue fork or cocktail stick, and let everyone dip their own fruit in the chocolate sauce.

A terrine of apples

Serves 6
Broadcast
10 September 1983

This recipe is based on a seventeenth century recipe for a 'pupton' or terrine of apples; it is a great way to use up windfalls after a storm.

1.25 kg/2½ lb cooking or sharp eating apples

75 g/2 oz brown sugar

60 ml/2 fl oz water

1 level teaspoon ground cinnamon

Peel and chop 1 kilo/2 lb of the apples and stew them gently with the sugar, cinnamon and water until they cook down to a pulp. Remove from the heat and mix in the breadcrumbs and egg yolks. Brush the inside of a 15 cm/6-inch soufflé dish with a little of the melted butter and stir the rest

3 egg yolks

75 g/3 oz wholemeal breadcrumbs

40 g/1½ oz melted butter

into the mixture. Peel and thinly slice the remaining apples and use them to make a pattern on the bottom and round the sides of the dish, sticking the slices to the buttered 'walls'. Carefully spoon in the apple mixture. Cover the dish and bake it in a cool oven (170°C/325°F/Gas Mark 3) for about half an hour, or until the mixture is set. Remove it from the oven and allow to cool. To serve, unmould onto a serving dish (it will be easier if you dip it in hot water to melt the butter slightly and loosen the edges with a knife) and serve it with whipped cream or yogurt. The dish can be served warm or cold.

Cherry clafoutis

Serves 4
Broadcast 14 July 1984

A *clafoutis* is a very popular French country dish of any fresh fruit cooked in a batter – a sweet version of Toad-in-the-hole or Yorkshire pudding. You can substitute plums or damsons for the cherries, but avoid the very soft fruits which go a bit mushy.

25 g/1 oz sugar

3 eggs

60 g/2½ oz plain flour, brown or white

60 ml/2 fl oz soda or sparkling water

240 ml/8 fl oz milk

325 g/12 oz stoned fresh cherries, preferably dark ones, or damsons etc.

40 g/1½ oz brown or white sugar

In a food processor or liquidiser 'whizz' the batter ingredients – the sugar, eggs, flour, soda water and milk. If you do not have a processor or liquidiser beat them to a smooth cream in a mixer or by hand and set the batter aside to 'rest' for at least half an hour before cooking the *clafoutis*. Pour a thin layer of batter into a flat pie or flan dish and put it over a low heat so that it just starts to set. Spread the fruit over the batter, sprinkle with half the sugar and pour over the rest of the batter. Bake in a preheated hot oven (190°C/375°F/Gas Mark 5) for 40–45 minutes or until it is puffed and golden (just like a Yorkshire pudding). Take the *clafoutis* out of the oven, sprinkle over the remaining sugar and allow it to cool slightly before serving, with cream if you like. It is also good cold the next day.

Old English dandelion cream

Serves 4
Broadcast 12 May 1983

Our forefathers could always find a use for the plants which grew in the garden, and that included the weeds.

3 eggs, separated

2 teaspoons rice flour

4 teaspoons ground almonds

¼ teaspoon each ground ginger, mace and cinnamon

1 tablespoon honey

8 dandelion flowers

120 ml/4 fl oz white wine

120 ml/4 fl oz cream

1 small sprig fresh, young rosemary, preferably with flowers, chopped very finely

Mix the egg yolks, rice flour, almonds, spices and honey together in the top of a double boiler or a bowl over a saucepan of hot water. Add the petals of the flowers (if you cut the heads off just above the base of the flower you will be able to peel off the outer calyx and be left with just the yellow ones). Mix well and gradually add the wine and cream. Cook gently over boiling water, stirring continually, until the cream thickens. Spoon into a glass serving dish or individual glasses and sprinkle it with the finely chopped rosemary. Serve it cold, but not chilled, with more cream if you like.

Hedgehog tipsy cake

Serves 8
Broadcast
19 January 1984

This was a very popular eighteenth century dish – and the more realistic it looked the better! We did our best to convince Douglas Cameron that our hedgehog really was alive, and complete with fleas. To prove it, I made some 'flea fudge' (see page 85) out of the fleas I caught while I was in the studio!

1 stale Victoria sponge or Madeira cake, about 20 cm/8–9 inches in diameter and at least 7–10 cm/3–4 inches thick

450 ml/15 fl oz sweet sherry or fruit wine

Cut the cake into a hedgehog shape, an oval mound with one end (which becomes the face) slightly more pointed. Cut a well in the middle of its back, reserving the piece you take out. Put the hedgehog on to a serving dish and fill the well with sherry or wine mixed with the brandy if you wish.

a little brandy (optional)

2 tablespoons apricot jam

1 large tablespoon grated chocolate

1 prune and 2 large or 4 small raisins

75–100 g/3–4 oz flaked or sliced almonds

300 ml/10 fl oz double cream

juice of 1 orange and ½ lemon

about 2 tablespoons castor sugar

Keep pouring the liquid into the well and over the whole hedgehog until it is all absorbed. Replace the plug in its back.

Spread the apricot jam all over the hedgehog and sprinkle it with the grated chocolate and use the prune to make its nose and the raisins to make its eyes. Then stick the almonds into its body, all facing slightly backwards from the head, to look like spikes.

Whisk the cream lightly with the fruit juices and sugar and either spoon it round the hedgehog or serve it with him.

Lime or lemon ice cream

Serves 4
Broadcast
18 August 1983

When someone kindly gave me an ice cream maker, ice cream suddenly featured prominently on the menu. Although this is a very rich mixture, the sharpness of the fruit prevents it being sticky – it's just yummy! You can use brown sugar, but it will darken the colour somewhat, and give a slightly different (but still delicious) flavour.

4 egg yolks

75 g/3 oz castor sugar

finely grated rind and juice of 4 limes or 3 lemons

150 ml/5 fl oz double cream, whisked lightly

2 kiwifruit, peeled and sliced (optional)

Beat the egg yolks and sugar in a bowl, preferably with an electric whisk, until they are pale and fluffy. Stir in the grated rind and juice, then fold in the cream. If you have an ice cream maker, pour in the mixture and churn-freeze as usual. If not, spoon it into a bowl to freeze, taking it out and giving it a stir once or twice during this time, to prevent the formation of large ice crystals.

Serve the ice cream in a glass bowl or in individual glasses. The flavour is excellent on its own but the addition of sliced kiwifruit makes it look particularly pretty.

Bob's coconut milk sorbet

Serves 8
Broadcast 30 June 1983

I have to confess to loathing coconut in any guise, but Bob Holness has a great weakness for it, so, to celebrate his return from holiday in the Caribbean, I made him this sorbet – which he said was delicious. When you buy the coconut, give it a good shake to make sure there is plenty of water in it.

1 medium-size coconut

450 ml/¾ pint warm milk

100 g/4 oz white sugar

3 tablespoons water

a pinch of cream of tartar

2 drops of almond essence

300 ml/½ pint natural yogurt

8 sprigs of fresh mint or a few flaked almonds, toasted

Puncture two of the eyes of the coconut by hammering a screwdriver or something else sharp through them and drain the water into a jug. Tap the entire surface of the coconut with the flat side of a cleaver, then split the shell open by giving it a sharp blow with a hammer – it may take several blows. If any coconut 'meat' sticks to the inside of the shell, dig it off with a knife, taking care not to break the point of the knife! Take a piece of coconut meat about 10 cm/4-inches square, peel off the brown skin with a vegetable peeler and grate it finely. Toast it under a grill or in an oven until it dries out and turns light brown, but do not allow it to burn. Meanwhile, break the rest of the unpeeled coconut meat into fairly small pieces and pulverise it in a food processor or liquidiser, along with the coconut water and the warm milk. Strain this mixture through a double thickness of cheesecloth or a double, clean J cloth, pressing the juice out with a spoon and finally squeezing the remains of the milk through with your hand.

Put the sugar, water and cream of tartar in a saucepan and gradually bring them to the boil. Bubble until the sugar is entirely melted, then take the pan off the heat and let it cool slightly. Stir in two drops of almond essence (more will overpower the coconut), the coconut milk, toasted coconut and finally the yogurt. Make sure they are all well blended. If you have an ice cream maker, pour the mixture into it and freeze for 20–30 minutes as normal. If not, just pour it into flat trays or a bowl and freeze for an hour. You will need to take it out every 20–30 minutes, however, and give it a good stir to prevent large ice crystals forming.

Serve the sorbet in glasses with a sprig of fresh mint or a few toasted flaked almonds.

Soft centre chocolate mousse

Serves 6
Broadcast
29 December 1983

The idea of this mousse is to use up all the violet and orange creams which are left in the bottom of the Christmas box of chocolates. If you actually like the violet and orange creams but can't stand the toffees, nut centres etc., don't worry: it works just as well with those but the texture is rather different!

225 g/8 oz assorted chocolates – soft centres, hard centres, liqueurs, toffees etc.

4 tablespoons rum or brandy (unless you are using liqueur chocolates in which case they will have quite enough already!)

2 egg yolks

6 egg whites

Melt the chocolates very slowly in a bowl over hot water, in a double boiler or in a microwave. Do not worry if the bits of nougat and so on do not melt – they add to the texture. Stir in the rum or brandy. Take off the heat and stir in the egg yolks. Whisk the egg whites till they are fairly stiff and fold them carefully into the mixture. Spoon the mousse into glasses and chill for at least an hour before serving, decorated with a few chopped nuts, or whatever seems appropriate.

Chocolate roulade

Serves 8
Broadcast
28 April 1983

Definitely not a recipe for the weight-conscious, but very quick to make, and an outright winner with chocolate lovers!

175 g/6 oz plain chocolate

5 eggs

175 g/6 oz castor sugar

3 tablespoons hot water

25 g/1 oz icing sugar

300 ml/½ pint double cream

Line a swiss roll tin with greaseproof paper and brush it well with oil. Break the chocolate into a double boiler or a basin over hot water and melt it slowly. Meanwhile, separate the eggs and whisk the yolks with the castor sugar until they are lemon coloured. Remove the chocolate from the heat, stir in the hot water, then mix the chocolate with the egg yolk mixture. Whisk the whites until they hold their shape, then fold them into the chocolate mixture. Pour this into the swiss roll tin, make sure it is spread evenly and bake it in a preheated, moderate oven (180°C/350°F/Gas Mark 4) for 15 minutes or until it holds its shape when lightly pressed with the finger. Make sure the oven shelf is level or you will get a lopsided roll! Once the roulade is cooked, take it out of the oven, cover it with a clean sheet of greaseproof paper and then with a wet tea towel and leave it for at least a couple of hours.

To finish the roulade, turn it onto a third piece of greaseproof paper, well dusted with icing sugar. Carefully peel off the lower sheet of paper – if you greased it well it should come off quite easily. Whisk the cream until it holds its shape, spread it over the roulade, then carefully roll the roulade up, by lifting the sheet of paper underneath and turn it onto a serving dish. Shake a little more icing sugar over the top. You can eat it immediately but it will be very 'squishy': chill it for a couple of hours to firm it up.

Pumpkin pie

Serves 8
Broadcast
24 November 1983

Whenever I have had pumpkin pie in America for Thanksgiving, I have found it fairly unattractive, but most Americans make it with a pre-prepared pumpkin filling. Although I am quite likely to be lynched by some of my oldest and dearest friends for saying this, I maintain that if you make it with real pumpkin you are into a 'totally different ball game'.

1.5–2 kg/3–4 lb piece of pumpkin

50 g/2 oz demerara sugar

1 tablespoon black treacle

1/2 teaspoon each ground nutmeg, cinnamon, ginger and salt

2 eggs, beaten lightly

120 ml/4 fl oz double cream

50 g/2 oz broken walnuts or pecans

20 cm/8 oz wholewheat pie shell (see page 77), baked blind

Ginger meringue: (optional)

2 egg whites

50 g/2 oz icing sugar

1 teaspoon lemon juice

50 g/2 oz stem or crystallised ginger, chopped finely

De-seed the pumpkin, cut the flesh from the skin, then cut it into large dice and steam these for 15–20 minutes until they are soft but not mushy.

In a bowl, mix the pumpkin flesh with the sugar, treacle and spices. Whisk the eggs with the cream and add them to the pumpkin mixture, then stir in the nuts. Spoon the mixture into the pre-baked pie shell and cook in a moderate oven (170°C/325°F/Gas Mark 3) for 45–50 minutes or until the custard is set.

For the meringue, whisk the egg whites with the icing sugar and lemon juice until very stiff and shiny. Fold in the chopped ginger and spread the meringue mixture over the cooked pie. Return to a slightly hotter oven for 15–20 minutes just to set and colour the meringue. Serve warm or cold.

Red fruit salad

I am a great believer in simple fruit salads, as I find a harlequin mixture of colours and shapes detracts from the appeal of the individual fruits. This salad is best served in glass dishes to show off its colour. If you do not have 'sundae' dishes, wine glasses will do just as well, although you may not be able to give such large portions. If possible, prepare the salad a couple of hours before you want to eat it, to give the flavours a chance to combine and develop. You can use any other combinations of red fruits when in season, for example, loganberries or redcurrants.

225 g/8 oz cherries, preferably dark ones, stoned

225 g/8 oz firm red plums, stoned and sliced

225 g/8 oz fresh raspberries or 225 g/8 oz strawberries, hulled and halved

2 lemons

2 oranges

Divide the fruit between the four dishes. Squeeze the lemons and oranges, mix their juices and pour them over the fruits. Unless the fruit is very tart you should not need any sugar. Serve the salad well chilled, with cream if you like, though I think this detracts from the deliciously fresh flavour imparted by the juices.

Strawberry tarts

Serves 8
Broadcast 9 June 1984

The special thing about this recipe is not the strawberries but the almond pastry – which can also be used with other soft fruit, plums or peaches, or pears in the winter. You can use wholemeal rather than white flour and brown sugar which will give a nuttier texture.

100 g/4 oz butter or low-fat margarine

150 g/5 oz plain white flour

75 g/3 oz ground almonds

2 level teaspoons castor sugar

1 small egg

4 tablespoons redcurrant jelly or raspberry jam, depending on how much flavour there is in the strawberries

juice of 1 lemon

about 225 g/8 oz strawberries, hulled and halved

Mix the flour, almonds and sugar and rub in the butter or margarine as you do for ordinary shortcrust pastry. Mix to a stiff dough with the egg. If you have time, chill the paste for 30 minutes before rolling it out to line a 20–25 cm/8–10-inch flan case or ring. (If you have pastry over, roll it into little balls and bake them with the flan case: they can be used for decoration.) Weight the paste with foil and beans and bake it in a hot oven (190°C/375°F/Gas Mark 5) for 10 minutes. Remove the beans and foil and continue to bake in a slightly cooler oven for a further 5–10 minutes or until the paste is quite cooked but not burnt. Take out and cool completely.

Melt the jam with the lemon juice. If the strawberries are well-flavoured, use the redcurrant jelly; if they are a bit bland the raspberry jam will lend them some flavour. Carefully spoon a thin layer of melted jam over the bottom of the flan case and allow to cool. Arrange the strawberry halves in the case, interspersed with the pastry balls, if you have them, and glaze the whole lot with the rest of the jam or jelly. If the jam gets too solid, reheat it carefully but do not allow it to boil or it will become like rubber!

Serve the tart with whipped cream, whipped cream mixed with yogurt or natural yogurt ice cream.

If you are using pears or any other white fruit, use apricot jam to glaze rather than the redcurrant or raspberry.

An Old English Easter trifle

Serves 6
Broadcast
19 April 1984

A trifle has to be one of the most individual dishes in English cookery – everyone has their own version, which they will defend to the death. Those who maintain that fruit has no place in a proper trifle do at least have history on their side. If you find the alcohol mixture too strong, mix either the sherry or brandy with a fruit wine or fruit juice.

1 large, stale sponge or Madeira cake

60 ml/4 tablespoons brandy

120 ml/4 fl oz sweet sherry

3 egg yolks

1 tablespoon castor sugar

240 ml/8 fl oz milk

120 ml/4 fl oz double cream

'whipt syllabub':

240 ml/8 fl oz double cream and 60 ml/2 fl oz milk or 300 ml/10 fl oz whipping cream

1 teaspoon castor sugar

juice of ½ lemon

flaked, toasted almonds, miniature macaroons or ratafia biscuits

Break up about half the sponge cake in the bottom of a glass or china bowl, mix the brandy and sherry and pour half the mixture over the cake.

Put the egg yolks in the top of a double boiler or in a bowl over hot water, stir in the sugar, milk and cream and cook the mixture slowly, stirring continually until the custard thickens slightly. If it looks like it might curdle, take the bowl or top of the double boiler off the heat and plunge it into cold water, stirring the mixture all the time. If you have a microwave, you can make the custard by heating the milk first and then cooking the mixture in the microwave for 3–4 minutes. (Check your own book of instructions for exact times.) Cool the custard slightly and pour it over the sponge in the bowl.

Break up the rest of the sponge and put it over the custard; pour on the rest of the liquor mixture.

To make the syllabub, pour the milk and cream or whipping cream into a bowl with the sugar and lemon and whisk it until it *just* holds its shape: it should not be solidly thick. Spoon it over the sponge and decorate the top with lots of toasted, flaked almonds, miniature macaroons or ratafia biscuits.

Baking

Sweet bannock biscuits

Makes about 12
Broadcast
22 September 1984

For people who do not like very sweet biscuits these will be perfect.
At first taste they are almost too plain, but they grow on you.

150 g/5 oz wholemeal
flour plus extra for
rolling out

75 g/3 oz medium
oatmeal

75 g/3 oz dark Barbados
sugar

2 teaspoons baking
powder

50 g/2 oz butter or
low-fat margarine

1 egg

3 tablespoons soured
milk or buttermilk

Mix the flour, oatmeal, sugar and baking
powder together in a bowl, then rub in the
fat. Make a well in the middle of the
mixture, add the egg and the milk and mix
to a soft dough. Roll the dough out on a
lightly floured board – it should be about
1 cm/½ inch thick. Cut out rounds with
either a biscuit cutter or a wine glass and
bake in a hot oven (200°C/400°F/Gas Mark
6) for 15–20 minutes. You should check
after 15 minutes to make sure they are not
burning. Cool the biscuits on a rack.

Chocolate and sesame biscuits

Makes about 15 biscuits
Broadcast 12 January 1985

These are for real chocolate freaks only: all but real *aficionados* will find themselves pulling out after only two or so of these immensely chocolaty biscuits.

75 g/3 oz soft butter or low-fat margarine

75 g/3 oz brown sugar

100 g/4 oz wholewheat flour

25 g/1 oz cocoa powder

1 teaspoon baking powder

2 tablespoons toasted sesame seeds

Beat the butter and sugar together thoroughly. Sift together the flour, cocoa and baking powder and mix them in thoroughly, along with the sesame seeds. Roll or squash out the mixture with your hands until it is about 1 cm/½ inch thick, then cut it into rounds either with a cutter or a wine glass. Transfer carefully to a baking tray and bake in a hot oven (180°C/375°F/Gas Mark 5) for 15 minutes; take care that they do not burn. Remove them from the oven, cool slightly, then transfer them to a rack to cool completely.

Oatcakes

Makes about 12 large oatcakes
Broadcast 26 May 1984

This must be one of Catercall's most popular recipes. Apart from the fact that the oatcakes are delicious as cheese biscuits, they freeze excellently, and do not go soggy when used as a base for cocktail canapés, for which we make a miniature version.

225 g/8 oz mixed oatmeal – fine, medium and pinhead

100 g/4 oz plain wholemeal flour

½ teaspoon salt

Put the oatmeal in a basin and sift in the flour, salt and baking powder. Rub the fats in as for pastry and mix to a stiff dough with cold water. Turn the mixture on to a board sprinkled with fine oatmeal. Knead the dough lightly, roll it out fairly thin

1 teaspoon baking powder

40 g/1½ oz each of butter and lard or 75 g/3 oz low-fat margarine

and cut it into rounds with a glass pastry cutter. Make the cakes whatever size you want, according to their purpose in life. Place them on a tray and bake in a moderate oven (180°C/350°F/Gas Mark 4) for 20–25 minutes, but keep an eye on them to make sure they do not burn. Cool on a rack and store in an airtight container or the freezer.

Yuletide cake from Whitby

Serves 6–8
Broadcast
15 December 1983

This is an excellent last-minute alternative to the Christmake cake that you did not have time for, or could not face making!

100 g/4 oz butter or low-fat margarine

100 g/4 oz wholemeal flour

50 g/2 oz plain white flour

50 g/2 oz dark brown sugar

1 teaspoon ground nutmeg

1 teaspoon ground cinnamon

75 g/3 oz raisins

75 g/3 oz currants

50 g/2 oz candied peel, or candied peel and glacé cherries mixed

50 g/2 oz whole, blanched almonds

2 eggs

4 tablespoons brandy

2 tablespoons double cream

Rub the fat into the flours as if for pastry. Add the sugar, spices, fruits and almonds and mix well together. Beat the eggs with the brandy and cream and add to the dry mixture. Beat it to form a paste then press the mixture into the bottom of a baking tray. Cut it into fingers or triangles as though you were making shortbread. Bake in a moderate oven (180°C/350°F/Gas Mark 4) for 1 hour. Cool, then break along the cuts into gooey biscuits.

Lemon brandy cake

Serves at least 8
Broadcast
8 October 1983

I invented this recipe for **L**emon **B**randy **C**ake for LBC's tenth birthday.

rind of 2 large lemons

150 ml/¼ pint brandy

3 large eggs

the weight of the eggs in butter (or low-fat margarine), castor sugar or brown sugar and plain white or brown flour

150 g/6 oz sultanas

1 teaspoon baking powder

Grate the lemon rind and put it in the brandy to infuse for half an hour. Meanwhile, cream the butter and sugar thoroughly. Separate the eggs and sift the flour. Add the yolks, one at a time, with a spoonful of flour each time to prevent curdling, to the creamed mixture. Beat thoroughly. Mix in the sultanas, brandy and lemon rind and a little more flour. Whip the egg whites until they hold their shape in soft peaks and mix the baking powder well into the remaining flour. Fold the egg whites and flour into the cake mixture and turn it into a greased and lined, or loose-bottomed, 20 cm/8-inch baking tin. Bake in a moderate oven (180°C/350°F/Gas Mark 4) for approximately 1 hour or until a skewer comes out clean.

Turn the cake on to a rack and cool. The cake can be eaten as it is, or it can be lightly iced with a lemon butter or glacé icing.

Walnut cake

Broadcast
25 October 1984

A splendidly simple cake which is quite dreadfully more-ish once it is cut.

75 g/3 oz soft brown sugar

175 g/6 oz soft butter, or low-fat margarine

3 eggs

Cream the sugar with the butter in an electric mixer until the mixture is reasonably light and fluffy. Gradually add the eggs and syrup, then fold in the flour, baking powder and chopped nuts, making

3 heaped tablespoons golden syrup

175 g/6 oz wholemeal flour

1 tablespoon baking powder

75 g/3 oz chopped walnuts

sure they are all well mixed. Spoon the mixture into a greased, non-stick, loose-bottomed or lined cake tin and bake in a moderate oven (180°C/350°F/Gas Mark 4) for 30 minutes or until a skewer comes out clean. Take out of the tin and cool on a rack.

If you like, you can ice the cake with a white glacé icing and decorate it with halved walnuts, but it scarcely needs it.

Shortcrust pastry

This recipe works equally well using white flour, which will give the pastry a slightly crisper texture. Wholemeal flour, however, will have more flavour and be better for your health. If you want the best of both worlds, use half of each. You can also substitute low-fat margarine for either the butter or the butter and lard, if you want to keep the cholesterol level down. On the other hand, if you're not worried about your waistline, you can make a really light, crisp pastry by using all butter and increasing the amount to 150 g/6 oz butter for every 225 g/8 oz flour.

These quantities will yield enough pastry for two 20 cm/8-inch flan cases, or to cover two similar size pies, or to make a pie with pastry top and bottom.

225 g/8 oz plain flour

50 g/2 oz butter

50 g/2 oz lard

3–4 tablespoons cold water

Cut the fat into the flour with a knife until the pieces are quite small. Rub the fat into the flour with your fingers, lifting the mixture and letting it fall back into the bowl so as the incorporate as much air as possible. Try to ensure that your hands are really cold and do not continue to rub if the mixture gets even slightly greasy; chill it in the fridge for half an hour and then finish mixing. It should end up like coarse breadcrumbs. It is better to under-mix than over-mix; under-mixing will correct itself in the cooking, too much mixing will make the pastry leaden.

Add the water and mix as lightly as possible into a dough. Roll out and use.

'Good brown bread'

Broadcast
30 April 1983

½ teaspoon dark brown sugar

½ teaspoon fresh yeast

300 ml/½ pint warm water (about 43°C/110°F)

450 g/1 lb wholemeal flour (preferably stone-ground)

1 teaspoon black treacle

a pinch of salt

Mix the sugar and yeast and add half the water. Put this in a warm place until the mixture froths – this will take 10–20 minutes. Put the flour and salt in a bowl. Mix the treacle with the remaining water. Make a well in the flour and pour in both the liquid mixtures; mix well by hand and then knead for a couple of minutes.

Turn the dough into a greased loaf tin, cover with a cloth and leave in a warm place for approximately 30 minutes; it should rise to almost double its original size. Bake it for 10 minutes in a hot oven (200°C/400°F/Gas Mark 6); then reduce the temperature to 180°C/350°F/Gas Mark 4 and bake for a further 30–40 minutes. To test it, turn the loaf out of the tin and rap it on the bottom with your knuckles: if it sounds hollow, it is done.

Wholemeal bran loaf

Makes 2 loaves
Broadcast 3 May 1984

This is a close-textured, quite moist bread – full of roughage!

25 g/1 oz fresh yeast or
15 g/½ oz dried yeast

1 teaspoon brown sugar

1 teaspoon honey or
black treacle

800 ml/26 fl oz warm
water

1 teaspoon salt

1 kg/2 lb wholewheat
flour (preferably
stone-ground)

75 g/3 oz fresh,
unprocessed bran

Mix the yeast, sugar and honey or treacle together in a small bowl, add 90 ml/3 fl oz of the warm water, stir around and leave for 10 minutes to froth up. Add the salt to the flour and bran, then add the frothy, yeasty water plus the rest of the warm water and mix well, using first a spoon and then your hands until the dough feels elastic. It should be slippery but not wet.

Divide the dough into two and either shape it into round loaves or put it into warmed and greased loaf tins. Cover it with a damp cloth and put it in a warm place to rise. If you have an airing cupboard that is ideal, otherwise the oven turned *just* on, with the door left open, will do. If the dough is heated above 50°C/120°F, the yeast will be killed and the bread will never rise! Leave it for 30–45 minutes, just until the dough has risen by half its own size. If the dough rises too much this bread will be crumbly and hard to cut. Preheat the oven to 200°C/400°F/Gas Mark 6. Put the risen loaves in the oven near the top and reduce the heat to 190°C/375°F/Gas Mark 5 after 15 minutes. Bake for a further 15–20 minutes (35 minutes altogether) until the loaves are golden brown all over and hollow when you tap their bottoms. It is a good idea to remove them from the tins (or turn them over if they are not in tins) for the last ten minutes, to brown the bottoms.

Preserves, confectionery and drinks

Runner bean chutney

*Makes about
2.5 kg/5½ lb*
Broadcast
4 September 1984

The idea for this chutney was given to me by a listener with a glut of beans.

1 kg/2.2 lb young runner beans, washed and sliced

450 g/1 lb onions, chopped roughly

350 g/12 oz demerara sugar

480 ml/16 fl oz malt or red wine vinegar

Cook the beans and onions together, either in a microwave in 2 tablespoons of water for 6 minutes, in a steamer for 15 minutes, or in a saucepan with about 2.5 cm/1 inch water for 10 minutes. Take from the heat and drain. Meanwhile, boil the sugar and vinegar together for 2 minutes or until the sugar is melted.

Make a paste with the mustard and

80

2 tablespoons wholegrain mustard

2 teaspoons turmeric

350 g/12 oz cooking apple, peeled and chopped finely

turmeric and a little of the vinegar then mix it into the vinegar. Add the vinegar mixture, with the apple, to the beans and onions. Stir them well and boil them together for about 3 minutes in a microwave or 5 minutes on a hob – exactly how long you cook them will depend on how crunchy you like your beans. Put the chutney in warmed, sterilised jars and cover them tightly.

Cucumber chutney

Makes about 3 kg/6½ lb
Broadcast
5 October 1984

The sharp and spicy pickling liquid contrasts well with the bland crunch of the cucumber – delicious with curries and cold meats, or in sandwiches at a picnic.

5 large cucumbers, peeled or not as preferred, diced

salt

450 g/1 lb onions, peeled and chopped fairly small

10 g/¼ oz mustard seed

25 g/1 oz root ginger, peeled and chopped very finely

10 g/¼ oz turmeric

2 generous pinches of cayenne pepper

1.3 litres/2¼ pints malt vinegar

5 cloves

5 peppercorns

350 g/12 oz granulated sugar or 14 oz brown sugar

Put the cucumber pieces in a large bowl, sprinkle them generously with salt and leave them for 24 hours. Next day, drain off the water and rinse off the salt. Put the cucumber in a large saucepan or preserving pan with the onions, mustard seed and root ginger. Mix the turmeric and cayenne pepper with a little of the vinegar to form a paste, then add that, with the rest of the vinegar, to the pot. Tie the cloves and peppercorns in a muslin bag or close them in a tea diffuser and add them to the pot. Bring the mixture to the boil, add the sugar and simmer gently for one hour. When it is cooked, cool it slightly, discard the muslin bag and then put it in warmed, sterilised jars and cover tightly.

Geoff's tomato jam

Makes about
1.3 kg/3 lb
Broadcast
1 September 1983

Geoff Gibbs, who sends out all the recipes requested by listeners, has a favourite holiday spot in Guernsey, where the tomatoes grow. One year he brought me back a pot of Guernsey tomato jam and challenged me to devise a recipe for it! Well, mine did not come out quite the same but it is jolly good.

900 g/2 lb ripe tomatoes, peeled, roughly quartered and cored

1 tablespoon tomato purée

25 g/1 oz butter

25 g/1 oz root ginger, peeled and chopped finely. If you cannot get fresh root ginger, you could use stem ginger

6 tablespoons lemon juice

the pith and peel of 3 lemons, chopped roughly

800 g/28 oz granulated sugar, warmed

some methylated spirits for testing the pectin content

Put the tomatoes, with the tomato purée, butter, chopped ginger, lemon juice and lemon rinds and pith, in a large pan – the mixture should not be more than 8–12 cm/3–5 inches deep. Bring to the boil, cover and simmer gently for approximately 20 minutes or until the tomatoes are quite soft.

To test for pectin (setting quality) put about ½ teaspoon of juice from the pot into a small glass. Let it cool for a moment then add about 2 teaspoons of methylated spirits. Swirl around, leave for a minute and then pour into another small glass. If the juice has set into a lump of jelly there is sufficient pectin; if the 'clot' does not form properly, or disintegrates when you pour it, add the juice and roughly chopped peel and pith of another half lemon and cook for a further 5 minutes. Repeat the test.

Draw the pot off the heat and add the warmed sugar. Stir it well until it is all dissolved. Return it to the heat, bring it rapidly to the boil and boil it fast for 15 minutes. Take off the heat, cool slightly and ladle into well-warmed, sterilised jars. Cover tightly.

The Colonel's orange marmalade

*Makes about
5 kg/10 lb*
Broadcast
24 January 1985

My good friend, the Colonel, has been making his own marmalade for the last fifty years and always expects to have at least two years' supply in stock. Several listeners followed his recipe and claimed that it was the first time that they had ever got marmalade to work.

1.5 kg/3 lb Seville oranges

3 large lemons

3.6 litres/6 pints water

3 kg/6 lb granulated sugar

Wash all the fruit, squeeze out the juice and pips and set the pips aside. Scrape the pith out of the fruit and put it, with the pips, in a muslin bag. Slice the peel – how thickly or thinly will depend on whether you like your marmalade chunky or fine cut – and put it, with the water and the pips and pith in their muslin bag, in a large pan. Bring to the boil and simmer gently for 1–1½ hours or until the peel is really soft and the liquid reduced by approximately a half. You must give it its full time otherwise it will not set properly.

Remove the muslin bag, squeeze it well and discard it. Add the sugar and stir until it has dissolved. Boil rapidly till setting point is reached, that is, when a little bit left to cool on a saucer wrinkles when you push it with your finger. Leave the mixture to cool for about 15 minutes, then transfer to warmed, sterilised jars and cover as usual.

Chardewarden, chardecrab or chardequince

Broadcast
13 October 1983

This is a medieval way of preserving fruit by turning it into a sort of fruit cheese. I think it is delicious and it makes a welcome change from after dinner mints, especially if it means you can use up all those redundant crab apples at the same time!

1 kg/2.2 lb apples, crab apples, pears or quinces

300 ml/½ pint white wine

2 tablespoons honey

ground cinnamon and ginger

Cook the fruit, whole or halved if they are large, unpeeled, with the wine and honey until they are quite pulped; this may take 40 minutes or more. 'Bray them in a mortar' – or purée them in a liquidiser or food processor. Sieve the fruit to remove tough bits of skins, pips and so on. Return the mixture to the saucepan, season to taste with the cinnamon and ginger and a little more honey or sugar if the fruit was very tart. Then continue to cook very slowly until the mixture is almost solid, stirring now and then to prevent it sticking to the bottom of the pan. This can take an hour or more. Cool the mixture slightly, then roll it or cut it into little balls or squares and serve it as 'comfits' or sweetmeats. It will keep several months in the fridge or longer if you pot it like a jam or fruit cheese.

Fruit and nut chocolates

Makes about 20
Broadcast
22 December 1985

These are extremely quick and easy to make (if you are really pushed for time you do not even need to coat them in chocolate) ideal for the last minute pre-Christmas panic! They will keep also for several weeks in the fridge although for longer storage, the freezer would be better. Either buy softened prunes, or soak for 2 hours before using.

50 g/2 oz pre-softened prunes or dried apricots

Chop the fruit and nuts with the sugar and lemon juice in a food processor or liquidiser

50 g/2 oz sultanas or raisins

25 g/1 oz dried apple, or figs, or dates

25 g/1 oz flaked or nibbed almonds

25 g/1 oz hazelnuts or walnuts

about 1 level tablespoon brown or white sugar

juice of ½ – 1 lemon

1–2 tablespoons brandy (optional)

175–225 g/6–8 oz good dark chocolate

until fairly small. Add the brandy, if you wish to be festive, and mix well. Taste the mixture and add a little more sugar or lemon juice if necessary. Melt about 2 oz/50 g of the chocolate and mix it into the fruit and nuts; allow the mixture to cool completely.

Melt the remaining chocolate in a double boiler. Roll the fruit mixture into small balls, then, with a tongs or two forks, roll the balls in the melted chocolate; put them on greased foil to cool completely. (If the chocolate gets too solid to work easily, add a little boiling water to thin it down.) Once the balls are cold, they can be removed from the foil on to dishes, or into boxes as last minute Christmas presents.

'Flea fudge'

Broadcast
19 January 1984

See Hedgehog Tipsy cake on page 64

120 ml/4 fl oz milk

225 g/8 oz brown or white sugar

a pinch of salt

25 g/1 oz chocolate, grated

2 tablespoons soft butter or low-fat margarine

40 g/1½ oz currants, chopped

Bring the milk to the boil in a heavy saucepan. Remove from the heat and add the sugar, salt and chocolate. Cover, bring back to the boil, then remove the lid and continue to cook, without stirring, until it bubbles all over; there should be tiny bubbles as well as larger ones. This is known as the 'soft ball' stage, and, if you have a thermometer, it should be at about 238°F.

Remove the pan from the heat and let it cool slightly, until it is just beginning to firm up. Then add the butter or margarine, beat well until the fudge is slightly shiny and then add the currants. Pour the fudge into a tray and cool. Before it is quite cold cut it into squares. Let it cool completely before taking it out of the tray.

Morning vegetable juices

Broadcast
21 February 1985

The idea for these juices was given to my mother by a Swedish doctor some years ago and gradually we have all become enthusiasts. Apart from being high in vitamins and minerals, the juice is very useful for anyone who suffers from constipation. Ideally the juices should be made every day, but since it is a rather messy process I find that it is more practical (and I stand a better chance of actually doing it) to make a big batch once a week and keep it in a well-sealed container in the fridge. The contents of the juice can change with the season but you should always try to include some of the following:

raw beetroot	raw carrots
tomatoes	some fruit

Nutritious fruits and vegetables which also give you lots of juice are:

green and red peppers	onions
radishes	spinach
cauliflower	turnips
grapes	apples

seasonal soft fruit

any citrus fruit, with the skin on

Leafy vegetables such as cabbages, sprouts etc. do not give much juice. You will need a juice extractor not a squeezer.

All the vegetables should be washed but not peeled, cut up and put through the extractor. You will end up with a wonderful dark red coloured juice. You would be wise to start with a fairly small amount until you get the combination of vegetables right for your own taste. Do not store the juice for more than a week, as it will start to ferment.

You can drink the juice instead of fruit juice in the morning, mixed with plain yogurt, or with muesli and yogurt to be really healthy!

Mulled wine

Makes
12 wine glasses
Broadcast
31 December 1984

A mulled red wine is always a good winter party drink – warming, welcoming, not too alcoholic and not too expensive as you can use fairly rough wine and brandy. Ideal for New Year's Eve.

about 10 tablespoons brown sugar

6 cloves

1/2 teaspoon each ground cinnamon, ginger and nutmeg

2 oranges, sliced

2 lemons, sliced

175–300 ml/6–10 fl oz cheap brandy

1 litre/1¾ pints red wine

600–900 ml/½–1½ pints water

Mix the sugar and spices in the bottom of a pan. Add the fruit, then the brandy and stir in the wine and water. Heat very slowly until they are *almost* boiling – do not boil though, or you will lose all the alcohol! Leave it to 'brew' for 5–10 minutes, then taste; you may need to add more sugar or spices according to your own taste. You will also need to adjust the quantity of water and brandy that you add to suit the party's requirements. Once you have got the basic brew made you can add to it, in the same proportion as the original mix, leaving a few minutes 'brewing' time after each addition.

Simply simple recipes

Most of the recipes which follow first appeared in a small booklet which LBC and I produced in the winter of 1983/4. We felt there was a need for cheap, easy to prepare but nourishing dishes for listeners who were not able to do much fancy cooking, but were aware of the importance of good nutrition – and who did like a tasty meal!

High on our list of priorities were pensioners living on their own, for many of whom cooking a meal for one is a difficult and un-rewarding chore. We hoped also to appeal to people of any age with major or minor disabilities; not only permanent handicaps but temporary disabilities, such as an arm in plaster, which could seriously hamper the normal range of movements in the kitchen. It also occurred to us that cheap, simple but tasty dishes might go down well with the young, fit and able who found cooking a bore but could not always afford the expensive prepackaged goods available in supermarkets.

The booklet was a great success, so last year we expanded it and again offered it to listeners who cared to write in. So good was the response that I felt justified in including some of the recipes in this book.

I would like to thank Anne Davies (who many may know from her involvement in the Sainsbury's Cookbook for Disabled People and her appearances on both radio and TV) who first awakened my interest in this area of cookery. Since she does all her own cooking from a wheelchair, she has been invaluable in advising me on what is and is not feasible if you no longer have total mobility or control over your body.

Chicken or turkey in a creamy sauce

1 chicken or turkey joint per person

a small piece of butter, margarine or lard

a small packet of frozen button onions in white sauce

Melt the fat in a saucepan or a multicooker and gently fry the chicken or turkey on both sides until it is lightly browned. Add the packet of onions with sauce and the milk. Heat gently, stirring continually until the sauce melts and mixes with the milk. Cover and simmer very gently for 30–45

half a teacupful of milk

100 g/4 oz (half a small packet) of frozen garden peas

1–2 tablespoons lemon juice

salt and pepper

minutes or until the turkey is tender. Add the peas, let them cook for a minute or two, then add the lemon juice, and salt and pepper to taste. Serve with rice or potatoes.

Chicken hot-pot and chicken rice soup

This dish can be made with chicken wings, which are very economical. If you like vegetables, put in two or even three kinds. This should provide a good meal plus an excellent soup for the next day. If you have a freezer you could cook a whole chicken, add more vegetables, seasoning and rice, and freeze what you do not eat.

1 portion of chicken per person

1 leek or 1 onion per person peeled and chopped roughly, or 1 tablespoon dried onion

1 stick of celery, 1 carrot and/or 1 parsnip per person, washed

a good pinch of dried or fresh mixed herbs per person

300 ml/½ pint (2 teacups) of water mixed with a little chicken stock cube, Oxo, Bovril or Marmite

a little sherry (optional)

1 tablespoon of rice per person

75–100 g/3–4 oz can of tomatoes or sweetcorn per person (optional)

Put the chicken, leek or onion, and the other vegetables (washed and roughly chopped or left whole) in a saucepan. Add the herbs, a little salt and pepper and the liquid and sherry if you are using it. Cover the pan, bring it to the boil and simmer for 30 minutes. Take off the lid, add the rice and tomatoes or corn if you are using them. Leave the lid off and continue to simmer for 15 minutes or until the rice is cooked. Season to taste.

Mixed vegetable soup

The reduced-price vegetables you get in supermarkets are ideal for this soup.

1 onion or 1 leek per person or 1 tablespoon dried onion

2 other vegetables (carrot, parsnip, swede, turnip, a few sprouts, a little cabbage etc) washed and chopped fairly small

a little butter, lard or bacon fat

about ½ pint (2 teacups) of water mixed with a little stock cube, Oxo, Bovril or Marmite

a small handful of chopped fresh parsley or 1 teaspoon of dried parsley

salt and pepper

If you are using fresh onion or leek, chop it and put it with the other vegetables and the fat in a saucepan. Fry them together for about 10 minutes without letting them burn. If you are using dried onion, fry the other vegetables in the fat and then add the dried onion. Add the liquid, bring it to the boil and simmer for half an hour. Add the chopped parsley, cook for a further 5 minutes and then season to taste with salt and pepper.

Lentil or dried pea soup

2 rashers streaky bacon per person

1 onion or 1 tablespoon dried onion per person

2 tablespoons dried lentils or peas per person

½ pint (2 teacups) water per person

salt and pepper

Chop up the bacon (with scissors if it is easier), put it in a saucepan and fry it gently. If you are using fresh onion, fry that with the bacon. When the bacon is lightly browned add the dried onion, the lentils or peas and the water. Bring it to the boil and simmer gently for 45 minutes or till the lentils or peas are quite cooked and mushy. Season to taste (you may not need any more salt if the bacon was salty) and serve.

Baked eggs in orange potatoes

Serves 1

If you have problems peeling the potatoes just clean them and leave the skins on – the mash will not be too smooth but it will have a nice taste. Or use instant potato.

100–175 g/4–6 oz mashed potato (about 1 large potato)

a little butter

juice of 1 small orange *or* 2 tablespoons orange juice

1 or 2 eggs

1 tablespoon grated cheese

salt and pepper

Mash the potato with the butter, salt, pepper and orange juice. Pile the potato in an ovenproof dish, make two hollows and break in the eggs. Sprinkle over the grated cheese and bake it in a medium oven for 15 minutes or a microwave for 3–4 minutes or until the eggs are set.

Pork hot-pot

This can be cooked in an ordinary pan, a multi-cooker or a slow-cooker; if you use a slow-cooker, follow its instructions for the cooking time.

100 g/4 oz belly or hand of pork per person

15 g/½ oz butter, margarine or lard

1 small onion, peeled or 1 tablespoon dried onion per person

1 parsnip or 1 small swede (or half of each) per person, washed but unpeeled

a pinch of mixed fresh or dried herbs per person

1 teaspoon flour per person

1 stock cube or a little wine

salt and pepper

Cut the pork into quite large pieces (leaving the bones in) and fry it gently in the fat until it starts to brown. Add the vegetables, either whole or cut into large chunks. Cook for a few minutes, then add the herbs and flour; continue to cook for a couple of minutes, then add the stock cube or wine with just enough water to cover the meat and vegetables. Bring the pot to the boil, then simmer it for at least an hour. Adjust the seasoning to taste before eating the hot-pot.

Anne Davies' shortcrust pastry flan made with oil

Serves 4

This recipe makes a short and crumbly paste which must be served from the dish in which it is made; its advantage is that it is very easy for anyone who no longer has full use of their hands to make it.

125 g/5 oz plain flour, wholemeal or white

a pinch of salt

4 tablespoons corn oil

2 tablespoons milk

Mix all the ingredients together with a fork to make the dough. Then put the pastry in the dish in which it is to be cooked; this amount will make enough to fill a small (about 6-inch) dish. Press the mixture out over the bottom and up the sides of the dish with your fingers and prick it with a fork. Cook the flan case in a hot oven for about 15 minutes. Cool.

You can fill the flan case with chopped, cooked chicken, turkey or ham mixed with Fromoux, Quark or a mixture of cream cheese and yogurt seasoned with salt and pepper and maybe a little lemon juice or a couple of drops of Tabasco sauce. Then eat it cold in slices for lunch or supper.

Stuffed breast of lamb

Serves 2–3

If possible, get the butcher to bone the breast of lamb and keep the bones for stock or soup.

2 streaky rashers of bacon, chopped with a pair of scissors

1 small onion, chopped small or 1 tablespoon dried onion

grated rind and juice of 1 lemon, or 1 tablespoon bottled 'real lemon' juice

Gently fry the chopped bacon in its own fat. If you are using fresh onion you can add that and fry it with the bacon until it is soft and just beginning to brown. Add the lemon, parsley, apple, breadcrumbs, egg and seasoning and mix it well together.

Lay the lamb flat and distribute the stuffing along it. Then roll it up carefully, trying to keep as much stuffing as possible

2 tablespoons chopped
fresh parsley or
1 tablespoon dried
parsley

1 small, tart apple,
peeled and grated or
just chopped finely
with the skin on

a small handful
of wholemeal
breadcrumbs

1 egg

450 g/1 lb breast of lamb

salt and pepper

inside! Either tie it up, or if that is difficult, wrap it tightly in a piece of aluminium foil so that it keeps its shape. Bake it in a medium oven (180°C/350°F/Gas Mark 4) for approximately 45 minutes. If you are using foil, open the packet after half an hour so that the outside gets nice and brown. You can eat the lamb hot or cold.

Aunt Vi's ginger biccies

50 g/2 oz castor sugar

100 g/4 oz self-raising
flour

1 teaspoon ground
ginger

a pinch of salt

75 g/3 oz butter

Mix the sugar, flour and spices, then rub in the butter (you could do this with a pastry cutter). Press the mixture into a swiss roll tin or something similar; it should not be too thick. Bake for 10 minutes in a hot oven (190°C/375°F/Gas Mark 5). Take out the mixture and turn down the oven to 170°C/325°F/Gas Mark 3. Cut into fingers and return to the oven for a further 5–10 minutes or until the biscuits are golden. Cool on a rack.

Hot posset or toddy

Serves 1

a mug of milk about
¾ full

1 egg

1 teaspoon honey

1 generous teaspoon of
whisky or sherry
(optional)

Heat your milk until it is almost boiling, take it off the heat and add the honey; then beat in the egg with a fork. Add the whisky or sherry if you are using it, stir and drink at once. If you are taking Complan or something similar it tastes *much* nicer if you make it with hot milk and a little honey.

Anne Davies' fruit cake made in a saucepan

25 g/1 oz (1 tablespoon) glacé cherries, chopped or whole

225 g/8 oz (8 tablespoons) mixed dried fruits

150 g/5 oz low-fat margarine or butter

a small can of condensed milk

225 g/8 oz plain flour, wholemeal or white

a pinch of salt

1/2 tablespoon bicarbonate of soda

Put the cherries, fruit, margarine or butter and milk in a saucepan and heat gently until the mixture melts. Allow to cool. Add the plain flour, salt and bicarbonate of soda, and mix well. Turn into a greased 15 cm/6-inch tin and bake for 1 1/4 hours at 170°C/325°F/Gas Mark 3. When it is done, turn it out and allow to cool, when you can ice it if you want, though it scarcely needs it.

Compôte of fruit

Serves 2

75 g/3 oz each (about 5) dried prunes and dried apricots

1 tablespoon brown sugar

a pinch of cinnamon (optional)

1 tablespoon sweet sherry (optional)

a large teacupful of water

rind and juice of 1 orange *or* a teacupful of orange juice

If the fruit is very dry, soak it overnight in cold water then drain it and discard the water. Put the fruit in a pan with the sugar, cinnamon, sherry and water. If you can, peel the rind off the orange with a vegetable peeler and add it to the mixture; it will improve the flavour of the juices. Simmer the fruit for 15 minutes or until it is cooked, then remove the rind and add the orange juice. Eat it warm or cold, plain or with yogurt or cream.

Index to recipes